EXIT PLAN

Mapping a Way Out of the Youth Mental Health Crisis

Dr. Kathleen Mackenzie

Get Ready to Evolve
Massachusetts
www.grtevolve.com

First edition: 2026

ISBN: 979-8-234-01139-8

Published by Get Ready to Evolve
www.grtevolve.com

Cover design: Jody Barna

Printed in the United States of America

Dedication

This book is dedicated to all the parents who have lost a child as a result of the youth mental health crisis.

Foreword

It's minutes before the highly anticipated coffee break—we're sitting compliantly in rectangular rows trying not to make it obvious the countdown is on. We were after all, seasoned teachers, clinicians, Principals and Superintendents who knew the sting of antsy and disengaged students. It was our first class gathering—each of us in pursuit of our doctorates in education.

Out of the corner of my eye, I spotted a tall woman made taller by her curly bun and perfect posture. The professor pointed to her—it was her turn to tell why she was giving up her well-deserved Saturday morning off to sit in a poorly insulated classroom. "I'm Kathleen Mackenzie, a school adjustment counselor from New Bedford". During her brief remarks, it became clear she was a woman of vision and passion for those she served.

Since our first encounter in 2009, Kathleen has continued to impress me with her signature blend of drive, humility, and compassion, and her adeptness in recognizing problems and mining for solutions long before they hit most people's radars.

You will see in *Exit Plan* that Kathleen is an eloquent writer. Getting to see her work as it unfolded, and to collaborate on projects has not only been an honor but has left an indelible mark on my own thinking. As we wrote our dissertations in parallel, it was common for us to be on the phone daily—deliberating, debriefing, and sometimes lamenting over the exhaustion we felt. But the day I picked up the phone it was easy to detect something more than the usual had gone wrong.

"Are you okay?", I asked.

"I lost my whole dissertation", she barely got the words out.

"What! Are you sure? You don't have it backed up?

"No, it's gone", she said dejectedly.

Months of devoted writing based on a lifetime of work had vanished because of a corrupted flash drive. Unsurprisingly, Kathleen found her way back to the computer with renewed resolve (and a new backup server!) Her mentor, Dr. Marlene Rodrigues gave her one of those heart-to-heart tough love talks that brought her back. None of us doubted she would. If it's for kids and families, hell would have to freeze over before she'd ever dream of giving up. Later, she received the Dean's Medal-the highest academic honor-- for the dissertation she willfully rewrote.

I'll never forget the speech that Kathleen gave the night she was honored with the Hubie Jones Urban Service Award. The room was brimming with social workers, and it would be an understatement to say she lit a fire under us. I've seen her hold the attention of many rooms through the years—leading professional development topics on every imaginable topic related to helping people thrive, to youth summits where she fervently handed out sleep masks to every student, and on public television on a sleep crusade to help underscore its vital role in protecting mental health. I've seen the way she listens, with care, and without judgment to the pains of parents, educators, and families who don't know what to do and cannot find the right help fast enough. This is the kind of person who needed to write this book, right now.

When Kathleen earned her doctorate, she joined the faculty at Northeastern in behavioral science and developed and taught a program in integrative health. I was fortunate to work in lockstep with her to develop a course on Stress, Resilience, and Behavioral Change—in which many of our students reported serious issues with sleep and overuse of technology, leading to many vital discoveries and strategies within the pages of this book.

Throughout *Exit Plan,* you will notice her proficiencies in teaching and understanding the critical role of sleep and technology on well-being. You will feel her heart the same way her students at the University do—she wants everyone to deepen their understanding of the problem and to become part of the solution.

This past fall, Kathleen was awarded an outstanding lifetime achievement award for her dedication to eradicating racism and empowering the community. It was a momentous time given that she had just formally retired from the school district where she devoted herself for the past twenty-seven years, first as a school adjustment counselor, then as the Coordinator of Clinical and Behavioral Services.

One of the driving forces of her well-deserved retirement was writing this book. As you are about to read, she has witnessed a concerning rise in emotional and behavioral suffering across each age level and demographic she serves that warrants collective attention and action. The minute she retired, she took herself to task—pouring over not only strategies she's seen work, but solutions with broad impact. She offers a skillful blend of diplomacy and directness for all of us—whether fellow educators, social workers, parents, grandparents, or concerned citizens—to avoid belaboring problems and roll up our sleeves to take much needed action.

I have had the great fortune of being inspired by Kathleen for over seventeen years—getting to know her personal journey and professional legacy from the inside out. I love how she starts the book by including some of her formative mental health challenges and how her own process of receiving treatment and endeavoring a life of service has allowed her to thrive. This kind of candor and well-earned compassion is evident through each chapter. Kathleen is a person who walks her talk and genuinely wants to share what she's learned to help prevent anyone from unnecessary and prolonged suffering. I am lucky to call her my colleague and dear friend.

Now, you have the chance to learn from someone who is a true champion for families, who understands the complexities at hand, and wants you to join her in finding the way out, together. I hope you will be heartened and motivated by her work as you search for ways to mitigate and mend the youth mental health crisis.

Kristen Lee, EdD, LICSW
Author of *Clean Slate: How to Make Change Happen*
Teaching Professor, Lead Faculty, Behavioral Science Northeastern University
February 24, 2026

Contents

Introduction

When Malcolm Gladwell wrote *The Tipping Point*, he popularized an idea that has stayed with me for years: when a segment of the population adopts something—an attitude, a behavior, a new way of doing things—and reaches a tipping point, it becomes much more likely to spread through the whole system. Once you cross that threshold, change doesn't just add up; it cascades. At the time, I thought of this idea in terms of marketing, social trends, and public health campaigns. I did not imagine I would one day be applying it to a youth mental health crisis that has quietly, then loudly, crossed that same threshold.

We are now living in a moment where at least one in five young people meets criteria for a mental health diagnosis, and many more are struggling quietly in ways the numbers never fully capture. This is no longer a theoretical tipping point in a business book. It is the child sitting in the back of the classroom, eyes down, who used to participate. It is the teenager who has stopped going to school altogether. It is the student whose chronic stress shows up in stomachaches, headaches, and insomnia long before anyone says the words "anxiety" or "depression." It is the "okay" kid whose grades are fine but whose sense of meaning, connection, and hope is quietly eroding. It is the family with their heart in their throat, not knowing if their kid is going to make it; and the families whose kids don't.

A tipping point can work in two directions. It can mark the moment something positive spreads—like a lifesaving public health behavior—or it can signal that something harmful has become embedded in the fabric of everyday life. With youth mental health, we have clearly crossed into that second category. The level of distress we are seeing is no longer a cluster of isolated cases. It is a social pattern. It is baked into how we are asking children and adolescents to live, learn, and grow up in this particular moment in history.

I have spent decades in schools, in counseling rooms, and in meetings with parents, teachers, and administrators, trying to help individual children through individual crises. I have heard the same stories, the same worries, the same sense of overwhelm repeated in different voices across different cities and communities. At first, it felt like a series of fires: We ran from one flare-up to another, trying to prevent immediate harm. Over time, it became harder to ignore the fact that we were standing in a dry forest, and the wind was picking up. What I once thought of as "individual cases" began to look unmistakably like a system on the brink.

That is why this book exists. Not because youth have suddenly become fragile, or because we have only just discovered mental health, but because we have reached a threshold where doing more of the same—more crisis response, more short-term fixes, more reactive services—will not be enough. Crossing the tipping point means this is no longer just the work of specialists or a matter of adding more counselors, as important as those roles are. It is now a cultural, educational, and policy problem. It is about how we structure school days, how we think about technology and attention, how we talk to children about success and failure, and how much space we create for rest, play, sleep, and genuine connection.

Over the past decade, the United States has quietly doubled down on treatment spending without changing the conditions that are making youth sick. Federal behavioral-health funding has roughly doubled since 2012, and total mental-health treatment spending climbed from under $200 billion to well over that mark by 2020. Yet during that same period, the share of adolescents experiencing a major depressive episode nearly doubled, the proportion of high school students reporting persistent sadness and hopelessness soared, and mental-health–related emergency department visits among children rose sharply. [1]. We are not seeing a return on investment in the form that matters most: fewer kids in crisis. Instead, we are funding a massive downstream response to a problem that is being manufactured upstream—by an attention economy that captures children's developing brains, fragments their sleep, floods them with comparison and violence, and then hands the resulting distress to schools and community clinicians to manage.

As I write these words, I am sitting in my home office surrounded by books like *The Anxious Generation*, *Dopamine Nation*, *The New Whole Child*, and *Magnificent Minds*. I feel a deep respect for the clinicians, social psychologists, educators, and researchers who are doing their best to respond to the rising tide of suffering. At the same time, as someone who has watched the youth mental health crisis unfold from inside schools and clinic rooms, I have had to face a hard truth: Despite many well-meaning efforts, we have not been able to change the trajectory of the crisis. Many people simply do not know what to do, or they are too overwhelmed, overworked, or under-resourced to act on what they do know. If we keep funding more of the same services while youth depression, self-harm, and school failure rise, we are not solving the problem—we are financing its consequences.

So how do we proceed?

I want to ask you to do something simple before we go any further: Take another look at the cover of this book and imagine yourself as the youth at the bottom of the well. If you have never rock climbed before, you might not see a way out. You might notice a few possible handholds or footholds but have no idea how to trust them or string them together. A more experienced climber would see something very different: a wall that is almost crowded with options, a sequence of moves that could, with effort, lead upward into the light.

As a rock climber, and as someone who has had to climb out of my own periods of mental health struggle, I see that wall differently, too. I see a way out of the well, and I also see a way out of the youth mental health crisis. I am not saying it will be easy; it will be far from easy. But part of my work in these pages is to show you where I see the handholds, why they matter, and how we might use them together.

Having helped thousands of youth and adults find their way toward wellness, this book is my attempt to clearly articulate a plan to change the conditions that are pushing so many young people to the brink. I will do this in two main ways. First, for those who learn best through stories, I will take you through my professional life as a clinical social worker in schools and communities. I will bring you into specific moments—classrooms, counseling sessions, conversations with parents and educators—and share what I was seeing, thinking, and feeling as the crisis grew. Second, alongside those stories, I will explain key health and wellness concepts so that the recommendations in the second half of the book make sense and feel usable.

Those recommendations are organized into three sections: a plan for parents, a plan for educators, and a plan for legislators and policymakers. Each section offers concrete strategies that individuals and systems can begin to implement right away, even while we work toward broader structural changes. My goal is not to place the burden of fixing the crisis on families, schools, or lawmakers alone, but to show how each group can play a powerful role in a coordinated, rights-respecting response.

My perspective is grounded in clinical social work and functional medicine principles, both of which focus on identifying and eliminating the root causes of illness. If you are more accustomed to a traditional western medical model, that leans heavily on symptom management rather than changing the conditions that create those symptoms, some of what I say may feel unfamiliar at first. I will do my best to make my reasoning clear, to share the science behind the strategies I propose, and to remain honest about both the possibilities and the limits of any single recommendation.

Gladwell's tipping point concept offers one more piece of hope that I want to carry with us as we begin: Once enough people see a problem clearly, once a new way of thinking reaches its own tipping point, different choices can spread just as powerfully as the crisis did. The same dynamics that allowed mental health challenges to become so widespread, our shared beliefs, our systems, our routines, can be harnessed to move us in another direction.

Part 1 of this book is written more as a memoir. It describes my professional career as a clinical social worker and highlights key events that have shaped my thinking about the development of the youth mental health crisis. This includes how youth presented before the youth mental health crisis, and the changes I have observed since the crisis began. Part 2 is instructional and presents the science behind the changes I observed in youth. Part 3 is the exit plan and is divided into 3 sections that include strategies for parents, strategies for educators, and strategies for legislators and policymakers.

By the end of this book, my wish is that you will feel more informed, more equipped, and more hopeful, not in a vague or sentimental way, but with enough concrete understanding and practical tools that you feel ready to join a collective effort. We are past the point where awareness alone is enough. Awareness has tipped. The question now is whether we will meet this moment with courage, clarity, and care, and whether we will choose, together, to climb.

Part 1

Chapter 1
From Locked Wards to "The Country Club"

As I sit in my home office, surrounded by half-packed boxes and retirement paperwork, I find myself replaying my 33-year career in mental health like a movie on fast-forward. I began my career doing crisis work and, in many ways, I'm ending in crisis mode. The difference is that when I started, crises lived mostly in locked hospital wards and emergency rooms. Now, the same level of crisis regularly shows up in school buildings across the country.

When I first stepped into the school system, it felt like a gentle landing after years on the front lines. What I didn't realize then was that I was catching the schools at the tail end of one era, just before the next one began.

Baptism by Fire

My clinical work started in a community mental health crisis center in the early 1990s. Almost all of the kids I evaluated had significant trauma histories—sexual abuse, domestic violence, or both. Many were suicidal. It was a baptism by fire.

A few months into my first year as a post-master's clinician, I made a mistake I will never forget.

I was evaluating a teenage girl in an upstairs office who was talking about wanting to take her own life. I'd done my assessment and was deeply concerned, so I went downstairs to consult with the psychiatrist about writing a Section 12, which is the paperwork needed to involuntarily transfer someone to a psychiatric hospital. The psychiatrist's office was near the front door. I remember thinking, *She can't possibly leave the building. I'm standing right here.*

With no one else nearby, I kept one foot outside of the psychiatrist's office to monitor the stairwell as I quietly started to explain my concerns. Suddenly, we heard someone shouting outside.

"She's on the roof!"

At first, I didn't process what that meant. I remember a half-second of confusion, and then that cold, sinking feeling in my gut.

She's the only client in the building.

I ran outside, heart pounding. When I looked up, there she was—standing on the roofline, hair whipping in the wind.

"I'm going to jump!" she yelled. "I don't want to live!"

My brain went into overdrive. *Holy shit. How did she get up there?* My eyes darted along the building until I saw it: an open window on the second floor.

You idiot, I said to myself. There was no time to indulge the shame. I had to get her off the roof.

I wish I could tell you exactly what I said to her. I'm sure it was some mix of calm-sounding words overlaid on top of sheer panic. This was long before my yoga practice and 33 years of breathing meditation rewired my nervous system. Back then my anxious brain did what anxious brains do: it fuzzed out the details.

I do remember talking slowly, trying to sound grounded enough that she could borrow the parts of my nervous system that were still functioning since hers was in collapse. I encouraged her to come back through the window and promised we would talk everything through. Somehow, she listened. In disbelief, I watched her climb back in through that open window and meet me in the evaluation room.

I was able to get the Section 12 signed and she was admitted to the hospital. Back in those days—1992, 1993—kids stayed until they were truly better. If that took a month, or more, that's how long they stayed. Given the time it takes for medications and therapy to work, a 30-day stay was not uncommon.

I remember spending much of that first year crying. After one particularly brutal week, I was sitting with my colleague Kim and said, "I'm not sure I can do this work. I can't believe what some adults do to kids. It's unthinkable."

Even then, I knew something had to change. Either I needed a different job or a different mindset. In the short term, I chose both.

At the end of that year, I took a job as a program director at a local agency serving women with histories of sexual assault and domestic violence. I supervised a largely volunteer staff of peer counselors. It was still hard, but the vantage point shifted. I started to see not just the damage trauma causes, but also the power of community and connection to heal it.

After that year, I moved to a well-respected children's and adolescent psychiatric hospital—a teaching hospital for a major urban university. I thought I was stepping into a more stable version of intense work.

I was wrong—and also, in another way, very right.

Life Inside the Locked Wards

My work at the hospital lasted for 14 years. My roles varied—I did intakes, individual and family therapy, and later took on-call shifts on weekends. When I was on call, I had to review every physical hold that happened on the inpatient units. Between intakes, trauma treatment, and restraint reviews, I was exposed to some of the most challenging behaviors in the state.

One of my most frightening experiences there involved a 17-year-old boy who came in for suicidal ideation. He nearly matched my six-foot height and clearly spent hours each week lifting weights. During the interview, he was surprisingly open. He spoke quietly about his thoughts and answered my questions without resistance.

Everything went smoothly—until I told him he'd be staying with us.

His breathing changed in an instant. His eyes darted around the room.

"No way!" he yelled. "I am not staying!"

It was the first time in my career I felt legitimately unsafe in an interview room. I had good restraint skills, but at that moment I knew I couldn't hold him. It wasn't safe to try.

I called a code. Three male staff from one of the inpatient units came running. It took all three of them to get him under control. At one point I saw the foam coming out of his mouth as they wrestled him to the ground. I was profoundly grateful I hadn't tried to manage him alone.

Later that evening, I went up to the unit to repair the little bit of rapport I'd built with him during the intake. By then he was mechanically and chemically sedated, and apparently still giving staff quite a run for their money. There was nothing to repair; he wasn't really reachable.

Scenes like that weren't uncommon. There were physically aggressive behaviors, of course, but also self-injury and what I came to think of as "distancing behaviors" where kids intentionally urinated, defecated, smeared feces, and vomited, to get you away from them. Behaviors that make it hard for people to want to stay close.

At one point, the laws around seclusion rooms changed, requiring staff to keep constant eyes on anyone placed in a time-out room. I watched kids climb walls to hide from staff in those tiny spaces. I saw intensely suicidal youth try to choke themselves with shoelaces or swallow pieces of their clothing.

It was an education on the outer limits of human distress.

And yet, over time, my mindset did shift. With supervision and training, I developed a specialization in trauma treatment. I watched children and adolescents, who had experienced horrific things, slowly reclaim parts of their lives. I saw resilience. I learned that with the right support and enough time, even very hurt brains and bodies can heal.

Still, after years of locked doors and constant crises, I started to wonder what it would feel like to work in a setting where not every child who walked through the door was in acute distress.

That's when the opportunity to work in schools appeared.

Entering "The Country Club"

When I transitioned into the school system, it felt like entering a different world.

No more locked doors. No seclusion rooms. No alarms blaring. People came and went as they pleased. Visitors checked in at the front office, but otherwise staff and students moved through the building freely.

Compared to the hospital, it felt like a country club.

I wasn't hired into the school department until late September, so the school year was already underway. My new principal was highly organized and ran the building like clockwork. Expectations were clear, and she held everyone—students and staff—to them.

I like systems and I tend to get my ducks in a row before diving into something new. So, I asked her to give me one week with my door closed to everyone in order to set up my office and my internal systems.

Thankfully, she said yes. So, I shut the door, rolled up my sleeves, and started reviewing the student files left behind by the previous counselor.

I braced myself out of habit. After years in a psychiatric hospital, I half-expected to find a stack of crises waiting for me in those folders.

What I found instead were students dealing with what I would now call "appropriate levels of distress" related to divorcing parents, an ill caregiver, some domestic unrest, or poor school performance. We also had a few kids with ADHD. Real problems, yes, but familiar, manageable ones.

There were about 400 students in the school. After hospital census numbers that felt like a reasonable caseload for one counselor. For the first time in years, I could imagine myself being fully effective.

It took me a little while to realize the 50-minute clinical hour I had lived by in the hospital was not the best way to maximize my service delivery in a public elementary school. That was my biggest adjustment.

Once I opened my office door and started answering calls from classrooms, the difference became very clear.

Learning the Rhythm of Schools

Over the next seven years, I learned how to be a school adjustment counselor, not a hospital therapist in a school building.

The school was what we called a "three-track" school—three classrooms at each grade level that housed grades K through 6. By the time I was transferred out, I was pushing in to teach social-emotional lessons to grades 4, 5, and 6 on a biweekly basis, using a curriculum I had developed myself.

In addition to classroom lessons, I ran weekly small groups, saw students individually, and attended every IEP meeting held in the building. At that time, school adjustment counselors were expected to manage all IEP meetings in addition to providing counseling. I was fortunate that my principal chaired those meetings, which freed me to focus on the clinical and logistical pieces of that process.

The kids—and the work—were different from the hospital, but not without challenges.

I remember one boy who was so hyperactive that I would regularly pull him from class for movement breaks, not because anyone wanted him "out of the way," but because I wanted him to make it through the day with some of his self-esteem intact. Ten minutes of walking and talking could reset him enough to finish his math or reading.

Another student, a five-year-old girl, came onto my radar when a behaviorist and I had to collaborate so she could be successful in class. Upon further exploration we found out her mother's go-to consequence was to make her stand in the corner on her toes for hours. We had some hard conversations with that family and helped them find more effective and humane disciplinary strategies.

We also had a boy who, when distressed, would head straight for the balcony railing. We occasionally needed to physically hold him to keep him from jumping. For many teachers, that felt like a full-blown emergency. For me, after the hospital, it was serious but manageable.

Those cases stand out as true exceptions. The vast majority of our students were relatively well-adjusted children, many from two-parent homes, who spent their days learning, playing, and occasionally needing a little extra support.

The leadership in this school also helped maintain stability and played a role in the school's overall success.

The Tiny Principal with the Tight Ship

Our principal was about half my size in height but could command a room like no one I'd ever seen. She was organized, decisive, and had high expectations for everyone in the building. Despite her moodiness, staff respected her authority.

She was also self-aware enough to tape a kind of "mood meter" on her office door. The choices were something like: "OK," "Caution," and "Beware."

If the meter was on "Caution," I might risk bringing up a medium-sized issue. If it was on "Beware," I made my best executive decision and saved any non-urgent questions for another day. On those days, I trusted my judgment and asked for forgiveness later if needed.

As firm as she was, everyone understood she wanted the best for her students and staff. Under her leadership, certain protective factors were consistently in place:

- Thirty minutes of outdoor recess every day.
- Few, if any, computers in the classrooms.
- High levels of parent involvement.
- After-school activities that kept kids engaged and connected.

Looking back, it's hard not to sigh with nostalgia. In general, kids were happy then. Staff members were busy but not overwhelmed. When a teacher called me to their room, it was usually because one child was having a hard time—not because the entire class was out of control.

Working in a school was a great way to regain a more accurate perspective. As a hospital clinician, it is easy to think all kids struggle with mental health issues because that is all I saw, day in and day out. Working in schools however, offered me a more global perspective being able to see the full range of strengths and concerns among youth; and perspective matters.

For a teacher who spent most of the day with thirty well-regulated kids, the one who was chronically struggling felt like an emergency. For me, even the most challenging student in that building looked nothing like the youth I had known in the hospital.

During the nine years I spent at that first school, I never once saw a child whose behavior resembled hospital-level care. A couple of parents maybe, one who needed hospitalization herself and one who looked like he lived on the street, but not the kids.

As a counselor, I felt effective. The work was intense, but I could see the impact of my presence. We had a school-wide incentive program. Parents showed up for events. There was a sense of safety and cohesion in the building.

It felt like the way school is supposed to feel.

Being Stretched Too Thin

When the district transferred me out of that school, it was one of the first jolts that reminded me how much systems matter.

For a few years, my schedule was split in ways that left me drained and perpetually dissatisfied. At one point, I spent two days a week at an elementary school and three days a week evaluating preschool children. Later, I was split between two elementary schools—three days in one building and two in another.

My caseload ballooned to about 700 students with no other counselor to support my students anytime I was out sick, which wasn't often.

Anytime someone asked how I was doing; my answer was almost always the same: "I can't get anything done."

For someone who thrives on checking items off a to-do list, that period was demoralizing. It wasn't the students. It wasn't the teachers. It was the structure. I was simply stretched too thin to do the depth of work I knew how to do.

Quietly, I worried that maybe I'd lost my touch as a school adjustment counselor.

Things began to change when a new principal came into one of my schools. Although she'd never been a principal before, she had served as an assistant principal in a middle school and had previously worked in the district as a teacher. She knew the community and was well respected.

It took her about a year to get her systems in place. One of her first big moves was advocating successfully to have me assigned full-time to her building.

That's when I started to feel like myself again.

Building a Kindness Chain

Once I was in one building full-time, I could finally bring the full range of my skills to bear. I trained staff in social-emotional strategies, restarted groups, saw students individually, and pushed into classrooms to teach social emotional lessons.

I also had the bandwidth to think about culture and climate at the building level.

One of the simplest—and most powerful—initiatives we implemented was the kindness chain.

Each grade level received strips of paper in a different color:

- Kindergarten: red
- Grade 1: orange

- Grade 2: yellow
- Grade 3: green
- Grade 4: blue
- Grade 5: purple

Together, they formed a rainbow.

When a student did something kind, they received a strip. They'd write their name on it, and sometimes the act of kindness itself. The strip would be stapled to others to form a chain in the classroom.

Every Friday, I took a student with me and walked from classroom to classroom collecting those chains. When I had enough from each room, I linked them together into a single rainbow chain and hung it along the walls of the main hallway.

By the end of the first year, we had covered the entire first floor in color. Over the next two years, we extended the chain onto the other floors.

Visitors would walk in, pause, and say things like, "You can feel the difference when you walk in here."

They weren't just talking about decorations. The culture had shifted.

Students held doors open without being asked. They noticed each other's efforts. When they had conflicts, many were willing to sit down in mediation and work through their differences. Acts of kindness became visible, tangible, and celebrated.

Although the school didn't receive the National Blue-Ribbon award until the year I left, I was grateful to have been part of the leadership team that helped the school achieve that status. The combination of solid leadership, consistent expectations, and intentional focus on social-emotional learning changed the building in ways people could feel in their bodies the moment they stepped through the door.

That success, I believe, is what put me on the district's radar for my next role.

When They Came for Me

I wasn't looking to leave that school. For the first time in years, everything felt aligned: a functional building, a strong leader, a clear role, and enough time with students to make a meaningful difference.

But in the background, the district's supervisor of school adjustment counselors had recently resigned. Several counselors saw me as a leader and recommended me for the position.

I had always thought about that role, but I also knew that none of my predecessors lasted very long in the position. In fact, we never had a supervisor stay more than a few years. I wondered, *Where do you go if it doesn't work out? Back to being a school adjustment counselor?* Maybe some people can do that, but I'm not wired that way. It is one thing I know about myself. Once I move on, I keep going.

When the central office came knocking, I looked around my beautifully functioning building and thought, *I've done what I can do here. It's running well.* Another thought followed quickly: *Given the emerging mental health crisis and my clinical background, I definitely have great qualifications for the job.*

There was a third thought too, one that I couldn't easily shake: *If I sit on the sidelines without being willing to step into the arena myself, what right do I have to complain?*

So, it was with genuine sadness about leaving an ideal situation that I decided to accept the supervisor role. I agreed to take the lead for all counselors in a district serving 13,000 students across 24 schools.

Because it took time to hire and onboard my replacement, I didn't officially start until the end of October 2019. That gave me about four months to get my feet under me in a demanding new position before the world, and our schools, shut down for COVID-19 in March 2020.

The story of those months—and the years since—could fill its own book. I'll talk more about that in a later chapter.

For now, what matters is this: when I walked out of that last school counseling office and into the district-level role, I carried with me three very different worlds.

I carried the locked wards and crisis codes of the hospital.

I carried the memory of an elementary school that functioned like a healthy organism—messy, occasionally chaotic, but fundamentally well.

And I carried an emerging sense that something, somewhere in the system, was starting to shift in a way I couldn't yet name.

I didn't know it then, but the skills I had honed on the crisis center roof, in seclusion rooms, and on elementary school playgrounds were about to be tested in ways I never anticipated.

Chapter 2
Fast Forward to Today

Before we dive in and unfold the development of the youth mental health crisis, I want to give you a taste of where we are today. During the six years I served as the district's clinical supervisor I saw what was once a predictable system become almost unrecognizable. What has changed over time is not just the students. It has been the environment they live in.

From this vantage point, I was not only able to see what was happening in my district, but I also heard about what was happening in other districts as well. I learned that conditions had not only changed in the last school I worked in, it was changing across the entire nation. I have spoken with several district-level administrators who state that "hospital-level" behaviors and significant concerns about child endangerment are now commonplace.

What does this look like now? It has gone far beyond students bullying each other online. Now we see students at every grade level injuring themselves, students overdosing on drugs obtained from strangers on Snapchat, physical aggression, suicidal ideation and suicide attempts at nearly every grade level, not to mention, an alarming number of school shooting threats. Counselors are barely able to service their students because of the number of crises that emerge on a daily basis, while a growing number of students are left to quietly fall apart in classrooms, hallways, and bathrooms.

The number of students, particularly at the middle school level, who share sexually explicit photographs with each other have law enforcement scratching their heads on how to respond to this growing phenomenon. They know these are kids who don't have the self-control or skills to think through the consequences, but they also know distribution of child pornography is a felony. Children and teens are now disappearing at a frightening rate. Those who decide to leave to pursue a "relationship" with someone they met online are the ones we find, sometimes. Those who have most likely been lured away by predators remain missing. And then there are those kids who take their own lives. We have lost too many to count.

And it's not just the kids. Adult mental health concerns are woven all through this story too. Many parents are overwhelmed and teachers and administrators are burned out or hanging on by a thread. Everyone is stretched past their limits, not just because of what is happening at school or work, but also because of things happening in so many families. If it is not a person directly experiencing a mental health crisis, it's their sibling, parent, child, cousin, friend, partner, employee, or supervisor.

Until this day, calls come to me from everywhere: "Do you know a therapist who's taking new clients?" "Can you help my son? We've been on a waitlist for 8 months." "My daughter hasn't gotten out of bed in a week."

Even as government agencies continue to throw millions of dollars at the mental health crisis, the need continues to grow. Waitlists are getting longer and the suffering is getting louder.

So how did we get here?

It's tempting to point to all the obvious culprits—political polarization, trauma, housing insecurity, the opioid crisis, financial stress, the pandemic. All of those things matter. They are real, serious stressors. But they've existed in one form or another for millennia. Wars, pandemics, economic downturns, and even genocides have never before resulted in the level of pervasive mental health challenge we are currently experiencing across an entire generation.

Based on my professional experience, something this widespread and progressive isn't just about individual stressors. It's about an entire species struggling to adapt to a rapidly changing environment.

Sometimes I wonder if what we're living through now is a human version of what animals experience before they become extinct—only in this case, what's at risk isn't our physical existence, but our ability to function emotionally, socially, and cognitively in a healthy way.

If I trace the arc of this crisis through my own front-row seat, there is one year that stands out.

It was 2017.

The Year the Tools Stopped Working

In 2017, I was still working in an elementary school. If I had been in a high school at that time, I suspect I would have seen the shift five to seven years earlier, around 2010-2012, when smartphones started showing up in nearly every teenager's pocket.

Because I was in an elementary building, the tsunami hit us a little later. But it hit.

Up until then, things were going fairly well. We had systems in place. The building was thriving. I had good, solid relationships with my students and their families. I'd been working with children for twenty-five years by that point and had a well-worn toolbox of interventions that, for the most part, worked.

And then, almost imperceptibly at first, the tools in my toolbox stopped working.

I began getting more calls to classrooms for "dysregulated" students. That wasn't new in itself—but the way these students responded to me was new.

Traditionally, when a student was upset, I could walk into the classroom, give a subtle eye signal or quiet cue— "Come with me, let's take a break"—and they would come. The relationship we'd built over time was usually enough to bring them along.

In 2017, that changed.

I'd walk into a classroom and instead of coming toward me, some students would run away from me. They'd dive under tables, wedge themselves behind cabinets, or bolt out of the room entirely. Others would just stand in the middle of the room and scream—high, piercing screams that went on for forty-five minutes, an hour, sometimes until they literally screamed themselves into exhaustion and fell asleep.

Some kids started hitting, kicking, spitting, or urinating when they were distressed. And I don't mean an occasional meltdown. I mean repeated episodes where it felt like the child had lost access to any kind of internal brakes.

What disturbed me most wasn't just the behaviors. It was the way they seemed to arrive without context.

Prior to 2017, when a student was upset, there was usually some identifiable trigger. Even if a kindergarten student couldn't articulate it perfectly, with a little gentle questioning we could usually piece together what had happened:

"My mom yelled at me before school."
"She took my pencil."
"I didn't get picked for the game."
"I miss my dad."

From there, we could do the work: identify the feeling, connect it to the event, and brainstorm strategies. Even with very young children, there was some ability to reflect on their experience.

In 2017, that capacity started to disappear.

I'd ask a child who was clearly upset, "What happened?" and get a blank look. Or a shrug. Or "I don't know." And it wasn't the defensive "I don't know" you sometimes get from a teenager who doesn't want to engage. This was a genuine not-knowing. It was like there was a short-circuit between the part of their brain that registered distress and the part that could attach words or meaning to it.

The other thing that worried me was that my relationships with students, relationships that had previously been powerful de-escalation tools, were suddenly less effective.

At the same time, another theme was emerging. Students were coming to my office saying they were "bored" in school with a frequency I hadn't seen before. They were distracted, inattentive, restless. And again, it didn't match what I knew of the teachers. No one had suddenly decided to stop teaching engaging lessons.

Yet the kids were increasingly checked out.

Smartphones, Gaming, and the First Puzzle Piece

Around this time, my fifth-grade girls started asking to see me because they were "depressed."

That language in itself wasn't entirely new—kids pick up diagnostic terms from the culture—but when I asked what was going on, I heard a new pattern.

"My parents took my phone away."
"I don't have my phone, so I'm depressed."
"They took my phone and I can't live like this."

When I asked more questions, they often described full-blown depressive episodes: crying all the time, loss of interest in activities, hopeless thinking—all directly tied to not having access to their smartphones.

Meanwhile, my boys' groups were being hijacked by endless conversations about video games. It got to the point where I had to build in "gaming talk time" just to have any chance of getting through the social-emotional curriculum I was there to teach.

"Okay," I would say, "you can spend the first five minutes telling me about your games. When the timer goes off, we're done with gaming talk and moving on to today's lesson."

Even with a timer, it was hard to rein them back in. Their bodies were with me in the group, but their minds were stuck in whatever virtual battle or mission they'd left unfinished.

I started to wonder if some of the boredom, inattention, and dysregulation I was seeing had roots in what kids were doing before they walked into the building.

So, I did what any good clinician does when confused: I went to the data.

I looked at academic performance, attendance patterns, and conduct reports. None of it fully explained what I was seeing. There were clues, but not a clear picture.

The picture started to sharpen when I began asking more detailed questions about students' technology habits.

"How much do you game?"
"When do you game?"
"What time do you wake up?"
"What's the first thing you do when you wake up?"

Student after student told me they were waking up early to game before school.

"I get up at four to play," one said matter-of-factly.

"And what time do you go to bed?" I asked.

"I don't know…maybe ten? Eleven?"

I remember sitting there thinking, *This can't be good.*

The more I listened, the more I heard about hours of gaming in the late evening and again in the early morning. Kids were flooding their brains with rapid-fire dopamine blasts from screens before their feet even hit the floor.

No wonder they were "bored" with the real-time pace of a math lesson by 9:30 a.m. No wonder they couldn't sit still. No wonder they were clinging to their phones like life rafts.

I thought I had found the explanation: early morning gaming was priming their brains for instant gratification and constant entertainment. School couldn't compete.

I began presenting this theory to parents during open houses and individual meetings. I would explain what I was seeing, how morning gaming and late-night screen time might be affecting behavior, attention, and mood.

I might as well have been telling them their parenting was on trial.

As I spoke, I watched their eyes glaze over. It was the same look I see when a parent is actively questioning their own choices but not ready to admit it out loud. I could almost hear the internal dialogue:

Is this really a problem for my kid? It can't be. I wouldn't do anything to hurt my child. Everyone else lets their kids have phones and games, so it must be okay. And even if it is a problem, I don't know how to change it. I don't want my kid to be the only one without a phone.

When they "came back" from that dissociative state, they often looked anxious and defensive.

Many said some version of, "We have a handle on it," or "I don't think it's really a problem." A few thanked me for my concern but clearly had no intention of making changes. Very few were willing to consider setting any concrete limits with their kids.

I could feel their fear of being judged as parents. I understood it. I'm not a fan of being judged either. But it left me in a bind. I could see the impact of tech use on their kids, but I didn't yet have a way to talk about it that didn't feel like an indictment of their love or competence.

So, I tucked that puzzle piece—screens and stimulation—into my mental file cabinet and turned my attention to another question I still had yet to answer: Why were students increasingly agitated, aggressive, and irrational, and why did they seem to have lost the ability to identify their own triggers or process emotions in a way that made sense?

That's when a nine-year-old boy taught me more about sleep than any textbook ever had.

The Day I Decided to "Nap" a Fourth Grader

One day, I got a call from a fourth-grade teacher who sounded frazzled.

"He's not responding," she said. "Can you come?"

She was calling about a student I had been working with since kindergarten. Over the years, we had built a solid relationship. He believed me when I said what I used to say to all my students: "You are never in trouble with me. I'm here to support you."

Even when I had to use physical holds to keep kids safe—something I tried to avoid but sometimes had no choice about—it rarely damaged the relationship. In many cases, it actually strengthened it. I think that's partly about how I do the hold and partly about how we process what happened afterward. Kids seem to understand when you're holding them to keep them safe, not to punish them.

So, I walked down the hallway expecting our usual pattern: I'd arrive, make subtle eye contact, give a quiet cue, and he would come with me.

When I stepped into the classroom, the teacher barely looked at me. She just pointed silently toward the second door in the room. Then she pointed downward, using a kind of universal body language for "underneath."

On the other side of that door was the back of the stairwell I had just walked down.

Okay, I thought, *he's under the stairs.*

I followed her cue, slipped quietly into the hallway, and approached the stairs slowly. Sure enough, there he was, wedged under the bottom landing, eyes wild, body coiled like a spring.

"Hey, buddy," I said softly. "What's going on?"

"Shut up!" he yelled.

I took a breath. "Come take a walk with me," I said, keeping my voice calm. "We don't have to talk. Let's just take a walk."

"I said shut up!" he screamed, bolting from under the stairs and diving under a nearby table. He kicked a box out from under the table toward me.

I decided to stay quiet for a moment and monitor from a safe distance—close enough to intervene if I had to, far enough not to crowd him.

The classroom door cracked open. The teacher slipped a stack of papers into my hands.

"This is the work he was refusing to do," she whispered, then closed the door again.

Schoolwork was the least of my concerns at that moment, but I took the papers anyway.

In the next second, he shot out from under the table and took off down a narrow hallway that led to the cafeteria. My heart dropped.

The cafeteria had two rooms and an exit to the outside. A dysregulated child running full speed toward an exterior door is every school counselor's nightmare.

I grabbed my walkie and called for assistance, hoping someone could get to the bottom of the stairs before he did.

You never really get used to that gut-wrenching feeling—watching a child under your watch charge toward a potentially dangerous situation while you're just far enough away that you can't physically reach them in time.

Thankfully, our principal happened to be available and responded immediately. She sprinted down the stairs toward the exit while I approached from the side. Between the two of us, we were able to contain him and escort him up to her office.

Once we got there, the intervention shifted into a more disciplinary tone, as it often does when a principal's office gets involved.

"You are supposed to be doing your work," she said firmly. "Now you're going to sit here and complete the work you missed in class."

She held out her hand for the paperwork. I handed it over. She placed it in front of him.

He immediately threw the papers off the desk and onto the floor.

"No!" he yelled. "I am not doing your stupid work!"

"For every minute you're in this office missing class time," she replied, "you will make that time up with me after school."

"You're the worst principal ever!" he yelled back. "I'm not doing it!"

The principal and I had a strong working relationship. We could read each other fairly well. I caught her eye.

"Can we give him a few minutes?" I said quietly. "We've just been running around the building in a cat-and-mouse chase. Maybe we let him settle a bit before we do any work."

She paused, then nodded. Her tone softened a notch.

"Okay, Teddy," she said. "We're going to give you a few minutes to sit quietly before we do anything else."

He began banging his fists on the table and his feet on the floor.

"No, I won't! I won't, I won't, I won't!" he shouted, over and over, rhythmically, like a toddler.

His agitation was rising. He was becoming more irrational, not less.

I leaned closer and whispered, "I don't want you to hurt yourself, Teddy. Let's see if we can get your body more relaxed."

"I won't!" he shouted, still pounding.

My mind flipped through my internal Rolodex of interventions like a card catalog on fast-forward. Deep breathing? He'd probably spit at me. Talk therapy? He was nowhere near reflective. Removing demands? The principal had already laid out the consequences.

Nothing seemed quite right for who he was and how he was presenting at that moment.

And then this odd, simple thought dropped into my mind:

This is a nine-year-old, but his behavior looks exactly like a classic two-year-old tantrum. What do we do with overtired toddlers? We nap them.

Napping a fourth grader in the middle of the school day was not in any evidence-based school counseling manual I'd ever read. It was definitely not in any district protocol.

I also knew that the mantra of the day in education during that era was "time on learning." The emphasis was on maximizing minutes in the classroom, not on napping kids in counselors' offices.

But my focus has always been to get students back to class as soon as possible in a state where they can actually learn. And none of my usual tools were working with him.

So, I decided to take the risk.

I picked up his papers and turned to the principal.

"Would you mind," I said carefully, "if I brought Teddy to my office for a little while?"

She looked as relieved as I felt.

"By all means," she said. "Go."

I turned to him.

"Teddy," I said quietly, "why don't you come up to my office for a bit? We don't have to talk or do anything. We'll just go there."

To my surprise, he scowled but got up and followed me.

We walked up the stairs slowly. I kept my voice neutral, my steps steady. When we reached my office, I closed the door gently behind us, walked over to the light switch, and turned off the overhead lights.

In the corner of my office was a small mat and a pillow I kept for kids who needed a cozy corner.

"You can lie there," I said, pointing to the mat. "If you fall asleep, I'll wake you in twenty minutes."

He walked over, lay down, and within seconds—before I could even make it across my very small office to my desk—he was out cold.

I set a timer for twenty minutes, knowing that longer might interfere with his ability to fall asleep that night. Then I sat at my desk, opened my email, and tried not to think about what I would say if someone barged in and asked why there was a sleeping fourth grader on my floor.

Every minute felt like ten. I knew there were a few people in the building who didn't think rules applied to them, including the one about knocking and waiting before entering my office. If someone walked in and saw him sleeping, I wasn't sure how I would explain it.

What if he wakes up even more irritable? I wondered. *What if I've just bought myself twenty minutes and we're right back where we started when he wakes up?*

Eventually, the timer went off.

I walked over and knelt beside him.

"Hey, Teddy," I said softly. "Time to wake up."

He stirred, blinked, and slowly sat up. I waited a moment for him to orient himself before turning the lights back on.

"How are you feeling?" I asked.

"A little tired," he said groggily.

"That's okay," I said. "Once you've been up for a couple of minutes, you'll feel more awake. Come sit at the table with me."

He got up quietly and joined me at the table. We sat in silence for a minute or two.

Then I said, "I'd like to see you back in class with your friends. Before we go, I'd like you to try a little of this work, just to make sure you're ready."

"Okay," he said.

I placed in front of him the same worksheet he had thrown on the floor twenty-five minutes earlier.

He picked up a pencil and, to my utter astonishment, started joyfully singing as he completed it.

His body was relaxed. His face was softer. The storm that had been raging not even half an hour earlier had passed.

I sat there, borderline stunned.

Intellectually, I already knew that quality sleep is one of the most critical variables in mental health. I had discovered this in my own life and recovery from bipolar disorder—but that's a story for another chapter.

Still, I could hardly believe that a twenty-minute nap could produce such a dramatic shift. Yet there it was, right in front of me: same child, same worksheet, same day—different nervous system.

I waited until he finished the work and walked him back to class. He slipped quietly into his seat and finished the day without further incident.

It was, up to that point, one of the fastest and most dramatic mood and behavior changes I had ever seen.

And I knew I couldn't ignore it.

The "Napping Experiment" Expands

I'm a data person at heart. An N of 1 is interesting, but not enough to build a practice around.

So, over the next few months, I repeated the experiment with Teddy and a small handful of other students who were showing similar patterns: intense, irrational agitation; difficulty processing emotions; inability to identify triggers; and that "two-year-old in a nine-year-old body" quality you can feel more than define.

In nearly every case, the results were similar. A short nap—fifteen to twenty minutes, in a darkened, quiet room—produced a striking improvement in mood and behavior.

Before that time, when I intervened with a dysregulated student, teachers might say to me afterwards, "Thank you for meeting with Susie. She came back in a better space and was able to get back to work," or "I appreciate your help. Joey had a much better afternoon."

Once I started napping students, the comments shifted and were noticeably different.

"Wow! What did you do??" teachers would ask. "I don't know what you did, but wow, what a difference!"

At first, I tried to dodge the question with humor.

"Oh, don't you know?" I'd grin. "I have a magic wand in my office."

But the results were too consistent—and too dramatic—to dismiss them with a joke about magic wands.

After the start of the shift in 2017 but before I started napping students, it sometimes took an hour or more to get a student calm enough just to sit in the principal's office for the rest of the day, and even then, they often weren't fully regulated. Once I started napping students, the whole intervention took maybe twenty-five to thirty-five minutes from the time I picked them up to the time they were back in class, and they typically had no further incidents that day.

I knew I was onto something.

I also knew that if anyone "caught" me doing it, I might be told to stop. Napping dysregulated students in my office was not in any handbook. Operating in secret didn't sit well with me either.

So, I decided it was time to widen the lens and bring parents into the conversation, not just about napping but about sleep itself.

That's when things got…complicated.

"He Sleeps Fine. He's Just Bored."

I assumed that once I explained to parents what I was seeing—and how differently their children behaved after a short, supervised nap—they would be eager to talk about sleep.

I imagined calling them in, asking about their concerns, and then saying, "Here's what I'm noticing. Your child seems extremely tired in class. Can we talk about bedtime?"

I also imagined them nodding in agreement and saying, "Yes, we've noticed that too. How can we help?"

That is not what happened.

Parent after parent told me, "He sleeps fine. I put him to bed and he sleeps all night." Or, "She's just bored in school. We don't see these behaviors at home."

Nothing they were saying matched what I was seeing in the classroom or in my office.

So, I decided to get more specific.

"You say Susie goes to bed without an issue and sleeps all night," I'd say. "What time does seven-year-old Susie go to bed?"

That's when I began hearing answers like, "Ten o'clock," or "Eleven."

I remember thinking, *This might be the issue. These kids are going to bed too late.*

"Why so late?" I'd ask.

Again, the answers were remarkably consistent: "She's not tired until that time. If I try to put her to bed earlier, she won't sleep. So, we wait until she's tired, which is around 10 or 11 p.m."

I flashed back to my own childhood, running around the yard after school, exhausted and in bed by 7:30 or 8:00 p.m. It was clear to me that something about kids' internal clocks—and their level of arousal—was different now.

But I still didn't have the full picture.

Parents were insisting their kids slept fine. I was seeing kids who looked exhausted and irritable. I knew tech was part of the story, but I didn't yet appreciate how profoundly it was affecting sleep.

As I was failing to convince parents that their children were sleep-deprived, I was still struggling to keep my student groups on topic and away from constant conversations about gaming and phones.

So, I decided to stop fighting their fascination and lean into it.

Opening the Floodgates

With each group I met, I started asking more detailed questions about gaming and tech use.

"What games do you play?"
"What do you like about them?"
"When do you play?"
"What's your favorite time to be online?"

Once I gave kids explicit permission to talk about their gaming and tech habits, the floodgates opened.

Student after student described gaming for hours after school and for entire weekends at a time. Many told me they stayed up late gaming in their rooms long after their parents thought they were asleep.

Others described waiting until their parents went to bed and then turning their devices back on.

Some said they woke up at 4:00 a.m. to game until it was time to get ready for school.

No wonder they were bored in school. No wonder they struggled to stay awake, to focus, to regulate.

They were either:

- Starting their day with hours of high-paced brain stimulation before school, then being asked to sit still and listen to a teacher talk in real time,

or

- Gaming late into the night, then coming into school in a state of chronic sleep deprivation, often shutting off their devices just before their parents woke up.

In either case, their nervous systems were completely out of sync with the demands of a traditional school day.

I started reading more about the neurochemistry of gaming and screens and how, over time, the brain can become less responsive to slower, more subtle sources of pleasure and reward.

Classroom learning, by comparison, moved at the speed of a human voice.

Even with this new understanding, I knew that "screens are bad" was not a helpful framing. Technology is here to stay. The goal is not to demonize it. The goal is to understand how to work with it in ways that don't undermine children's basic biological needs.

At that point, I suspected tech and sleep were deeply intertwined. I had seen dramatic transformations in a handful of students with short naps and earlier bedtimes. I still needed more evidence.

That's when a first grader who cried all day showed me another piece of the puzzle.

The First Grader Who Cried All Day

It was October when we got a new student in first grade. He was new to the United States and didn't speak a word of English.

From day one, he cried all day long.

Not intermittent crying. Not "I'm having a bad morning" crying. Nonstop, full-volume crying.

His teacher tried everything she could think of. She paired him with Spanish-speaking peers. She showed him where things were, offered reassurance, and gave him space.

Nothing helped.

Very quickly, I was called in.

I went to the classroom, gently took his hand, and walked him to my office. He cried the entire way. I thought, *Maybe if I speak to him in Spanish, he'll feel more at ease.*

I greeted him warmly in Spanish, showed him the toys in my office, and offered him a snack. I tried sitting quietly so he could see I wasn't going to push him.

He cried through all of it. Loudly. He was so upset I doubt he heard a word I said.

At a loss, I brought him back to class and suggested the teacher continue pairing him with Spanish-speaking peers. Feeling defeated, I wished her good luck and went on with my day.

Every time I walked past the classroom that week, I could hear him crying.

By the end of the week, I decided, *Okay, there has to be more going on here. Time to call in the parents.*

I arranged for them to meet with me the following Monday.

They arrived on time and we met in my office. I greeted them in Spanish and took a thorough family history, including questions about their lives in Central America and their journey to the United States.

Based on my experience with many students from Central America—Guatemala, El Salvador, Honduras—I was well aware of the level of trauma some families endure. I had heard stories of gangs cutting off fingers just to remove the rings they carried and entire families being shot and killed while sitting in their car. Our school was a receiving school for newcomers with limited English proficiency; their stories had taught me a lot.

So, my first thought as I met with this boy's parents was, *There must be a trauma history.*

But the story his parents told was uneventful. No major losses. No violent incidents. No dangerous journey. Nothing that connected cleanly to his nonstop crying in school.

As we talked, I noticed both parents yawning. Not once or twice, but repeatedly.

I realized that, in my own bias toward assuming trauma—because so many of our students from Central America had it—I had skipped one of the first questions I usually ask when I meet with parents:

"How is he sleeping?"

Seeing the yawns jogged my memory.

"I notice both of you are yawning," I said gently. "What time does your son go to bed?"

"Ten or eleven," they answered.

"Why so late?" I asked, expecting to hear the now-familiar response of "He's not tired until then."

Instead, they said, "That's what time we all go to bed."

I felt a small surge of hope.

"I'm going to give you some of your adult time back," I told them, smiling. "Would you consider putting him to bed at 7:30 from now on? You'll get your evenings back, and you might sleep better yourselves too."

They looked at each other, nodded, and agreed.

The next day, I waited at the front door to greet him and see how his night went. To my delight, he entered the school smiling ear to ear.

Throughout the day he was cheerful and engaged with his peers. He affectionately hugged his teacher and other adults in the building. The nonstop crying had vanished overnight. He was the same child, but in a different body, or at least in a different physiological state.

Aside from Teddy, this was one of the most dramatic single-day changes I'd ever seen as a result of adequate sleep.

By then, the pattern was becoming impossible to ignore:

- Highly dysregulated child
- Short or inadequate sleep
- Strategic change in sleep pattern
- Dramatic improvement in behavior and mood

It wasn't every child, of course. Not every case was that simple. But there were enough of these stories now that I knew sleep was a key lever.

The question was: how far did it go? How many of the kids we were labeling as "oppositional," "defiant," "anxious," or "depressed" were actually profoundly sleep-deprived?

And what would it take to get adults—parents, educators, leaders—to take sleep seriously enough to help kids change?

Those questions took me down a path that turned out to be deeply personal. Because as I watched my students transform with naps and earlier bedtimes, I couldn't help but think of my own nervous system—the one that had once unraveled so spectacularly it had landed me in a psychiatric hospital years ago as a young adult.

I had seen what happens to a child's brain when you restore sleep.

I knew, from lived experience, what happens to an adult brain when you don't.

In the next chapter, I'll share that part of the story—not because I like talking about myself, but because my story is a powerful one and may further add to understanding what happens to a human being when sleep, stress, and environment collide in just the wrong way.

Chapter 3
Sleep, Screens, and a System on the Brink

As I watched nine-year-old kids transform after a twenty-minute nap on the floor of my office, I couldn't help thinking about my own brain and how spectacularly it had come undone years earlier.

I had been watching students go from wild-eyed, unreachable, and irrational to calm, cooperative, and even joyful after nothing more than a short, protected rest and an earlier bedtime. I could see the difference in their faces, their bodies, their schoolwork. It was right in front of me.

And my nervous system kept whispering, *You've seen this before. In here.*

By "in here," I meant my own mind.

Before I ever worked in a psychiatric hospital or walked into an elementary school, I had been a patient myself.

The Night Everything Changed

In 1989, I was abducted from my apartment.

I mention this one detail because trauma is now a word that is often used inaccurately. I provide it so you know I am talking about a big T trauma by anyone's definition. In the interest of not wanting to vicariously traumatize anyone reading this, I will just say that I was able to escape fairly quickly, but not without significant consequences to my mental health.

In the aftermath, I unraveled.

I stopped sleeping. My thoughts raced. My moods ricocheted between euphoria and despair. At first, I tried to muscle through it, but my mind wasn't interested in being muscled. It had its own agenda.

Eventually, I was hospitalized for thirty days. I was diagnosed with manic depression, now called bipolar disorder. The diagnosis was accurate, but my treatment was complicated by the trauma.

It took five years of medication changes and trauma therapy before I stabilized.

It was not for lack of effort on my part. For six months, I lived in my parents' basement reading psychology books and going to therapy, trying to make sense of what was happening to me. I wanted to understand it from the inside out.

Then I did something that probably won't surprise you if you've read this far: I went to school.

I enrolled in a master's program in clinical social work.

If I couldn't immediately fix my brain, I at least wanted to understand what was happening inside it. Graduate school became both my coping strategy and my way of reclaiming some control.

Once I stabilized, I remained on medication for about twenty years.

I didn't love the idea of being on meds for the rest of my life, but I accepted it as the best option available. I had been very sick. I knew what it felt like to lose my footing completely, and I had no desire to repeat that experience.

But even on medication, my mood and energy still fluctuated. There were stretches where I didn't feel great, and it didn't fully make sense to me that things could vary to the degree that it did if the medication was the main thing keeping me stable.

That curiosity—maybe stubbornness—is what eventually led me to learn about the fields of epigenetics, sleep science, and a completely different way of thinking about mental health.

Epigenetics, Data, and a Different Kind of Experiment

At some point along the way, the person I was living with observed what I now consider one of the most important clinical insights of my life.

"You do better," he said, "when you get enough sleep."

It was such a simple statement, and also annoyingly obvious in hindsight. But at the time, it landed with surprising force. I started paying closer attention.

This was before Apple Watches and Oura rings, so I tracked everything on paper: how long I slept, what time I went to bed, my menstrual cycles, my stress levels, anything I thought might matter. I was my own little research study.

As technology evolved, my tracking went digital. I got an Oura ring to monitor sleep, energy, heart rate variability among other variables. At times I've worn a continuous glucose monitor, even though I don't have diabetes, just to see how food, stress, and sleep interacted in my body.

None of this was about perfection. It was about curiosity. Every new data point suggested that I had more influence over my mental health than I had originally been taught.

Around the same time, I stumbled onto the field of epigenetics and the work of Dr. Bruce Lipton [2]. He describes an experiment where he took a single stem cell and allowed it to divide in a petri dish until there were many genetically identical cells. He then divided those cells into three different dishes and changed the environment in each one.

In one dish, the cells became muscle cells.
In another, bone cells.
In the third, fat cells.

Same DNA. Different environments. Completely different outcomes.

That experiment among others was, to the best of my knowledge, what led to the birth of epigenetics as a field of researchers studying how our environment influences gene expression. More recent research suggests that as much as 80 percent of our genetic expression is driven by the environment, and only about 20 percent is determined by the genes we're born with [3].

When I learned this, I remember thinking, *If the environment is that powerful, I wonder if I can create an internal environment where the "expression" of bipolar disorder just isn't supported.*

That question sat in the back of my mind for a long time.

Around then I also read Aspen Morrow's book *Med-Free Bipolar* [4], and later, Dr. Matthew Walker's *Why We Sleep* [5]. Walker's book, in particular, blew my mind. Up until then, I knew sleep was "important," but I had no idea how many systems depended on it—emotional regulation, learning, memory consolidation, immune function, and metabolic health among others. The more I learned, the more I saw my own history in its pages.

At some point, my curiosity, my data, and my lived experience converged.

I decided to try an experiment.

I implemented all the strategies I had been learning about over time. I stabilized my environment through a consistent sleep schedule, high-quality nutrition, regular exercise, and stress management. I treated my body like the petri dish in Lipton's experiment, trying to make it a place where stability was more likely than chaos.

Once I had maintained that consistency for a long while, I felt confident in how to support my body to maintain stability. I am now fully recovered from bipolar disorder and have been able to maintain my stability despite the following stressors:

- Buying my first independently-owned house.
- Taking on a demanding administrative position that required me to guide an entire school district of counselors and related service professionals through a pandemic.

- Welcoming my elderly parents permanently into my home within two weeks of inviting them to live with me, so I could support my mother in caring for my father with dementia.

My moods have remained stable through all these stressors, and the catastrophic swings that once landed me in the hospital have not returned. Don't get me wrong, I still have my moments, because I'm a human being, not a robot, but consistent sleep and other lifestyle factors have been the most powerful stabilizers for me.

So, by the time I was napping fourth graders in my office and watching first graders transform overnight with an earlier bedtime, I wasn't just seeing "good interventions."

I was seeing a pattern I recognized in my bones.

When you give the brain adequate sleep and a more regulated environment, everything else gets easier.

The question was: could we bring that understanding to scale inside a public-school system that was, at the same time, becoming more and more entangled with technology?

A Digital Reform Movement That Never Happened

When I stepped into the district-wide supervisor role in late October 2019, I was brimming with ideas. High on my list was a district-wide initiative addressing problematic technology use.

After years of watching individual families struggle with phone and gaming boundaries, and after seeing those early signs of tech-related dysregulation in students, I wanted to move upstream. I imagined a campaign that would educate staff, parents, and students about digital health, set reasonable tech limits in school, and support families in setting them at home.

I called it, in my head, the digital reform movement.

What I didn't fully appreciate at the time was just how deeply many districts were already invested in ramping up technology.

When I floated concerns about tech overuse by my colleagues, I got the same glazed look I had seen from parents.

If I could have read their minds, I imagine I would have heard something like:

How can we pull back on tech usage now? Everything we do is online. Other districts are doing the same; it must be fine. We've already spent the money. The train has left the station.

The digital reform movement was dead before it began.

I filed that away under "things to come back to later" and focused on getting my feet under me in the new job.

I had about four months before the floor fell out from under my feet.

"Let's Have Some Guts and Stay Open"

In March of 2020, I remember walking down the hallway with one of the other administrators, talking about this new virus that was starting to dominate the news.

"What do you think is going to happen?" he asked.

"I don't know," I said, "but I hope we have the guts to stay open. The kids need to be in school."

I really believed that. I still believe that schools, done well, are one of our best protective factors for kids, especially those who don't have consistency at home.

By the end of that week, we all got the message: *Do not report back to work or school for the next two weeks.*

Since my partner lives in another state, I immediately booked a flight to see him and planned to stay for the full two weeks. As we sat in his living room watching the news, it became less and less clear whether flights would continue. There was talk of shutting airports down altogether.

I cut my visit short and flew home early, worried I might not be able to get back if I waited. Of course, those "two weeks" turned into the rest of the school year. None of us returned to our buildings, and we all had to learn, very quickly, how to work from home.

Thankfully, I had already been teaching remotely at the university level, and I was managing a long-distance relationship, so I wasn't completely new to Zoom or online communication. But for many of the counselors and related service providers I supervised, it was their first real immersion into telehealth.

It was an extremely challenging year.

Many counselors couldn't reach the students on their caseloads at all. Phone numbers were disconnected. Email addresses bounced. Families were overwhelmed, transient, or both.

When they did reach students, it was often to find them holed up in dark bedrooms with the blinds closed, scrolling on their phones or sleeping most of the day away. Some had their cameras off and refused to turn them on. For others, a major therapeutic accomplishment was seeing them open their blinds.

We weren't talking about deep trauma work. We were talking about coaxing a teenager to let some sunlight into the room.

The Empty World

Outside my own four walls, the world felt eerily empty.

I started taking daily walks outside because gyms were closed and frankly, my sanity depended on it. At first, I expected to see other walkers, kids on bikes, and families in yards.

What I saw instead were deserted streets.

Even on holiday weekends or school vacations, no one was out. Parks were empty. Playgrounds were taped off. Basketball hoops were removed or chained up. It felt like a movie set after everyone had gone home.

Travel was just as surreal. Once airports began operating again in limited fashion, I took occasional flights to see my partner. I took pictures of cavernous terminals with no people in them, escalators with one lone traveler, and that lone traveler was usually just me.

I remember standing in one nearly empty terminal, looking around and thinking, *This is the kind of scene we used to only see in films. I feel like I am living through an Apocalypse.*

There was no doubt in my mind that the messaging being sent to the public—some of it necessary, some of it arguably not—had scared the crap out of everyone.

As I walked through empty parks, ghost towns, and cavernous airports, I thought about our students. *What the heck's going to happen when we try to bring them back?*

The Students Who Never Came Back

The following September, our district decided to offer in-person schooling to our students with special education needs, while the rest of the students continued learning remotely.

Many teachers protested the return. They were worried that students would refuse to wear masks, that social distancing wouldn't be possible, and that we would all be at risk.

In the end, the kids did better with the rules than many adults had predicted. The students who attended school seemed to understand that the situation we all were in was serious. For the most part, they complied with masks and social distancing protocols.

It was obvious, though, that the students had been dramatically affected.

Their academic skills had regressed. Their social skills had, too. There was a palpable awkwardness when they tried to interact with each other. Things that used to be automatic—sharing space, taking turns, reading facial expressions—were rusty. Really rusty!

The real eye-opener came later, when we invited all the students back for in-person learning.

Some came right in. A significant number did not.

It took coordinated efforts by school staff, attendance officers, and sometimes even police liaisons to get certain students back into the building. As of this writing, there are still students who never fully returned to in-person learning. Many are out due to social phobia, school anxiety, or debilitating depression.

This wasn't just my district. Colleagues from around the state and across the country reported the same pattern: a "missing middle" of students who hadn't dropped out officially but were effectively gone.

Once everyone was technically "back," the fallout from the pandemic was now in full color and no one was prepared for what happened next. The schools were immediately under distress, but those distress signals rarely reached the district level in real time. The staff in each building were too busy managing the chaos in front of them.

But the stories about what was happening in schools were getting around, whether it was through someone at the schools, from administrators in other districts or via news outlets from around the country. Reports of extreme violence and very unsafe conditions were quickly becoming news—so extreme that one district in our state requested help from the National Guard. There were also the now-familiar headlines about school shootings and other threats to schools.

Even though no one was calling me directly to ask for help, the rumor mill, which was alive and well, sparked too much curiosity in me to remain a bystander.

So, one day, I decided to go see for myself.

The Other Side of the Glass

The morning I chose to visit one of the high schools, I found myself standing in front of my dresser, staring into space when suddenly a thought flashed across my mind: *I could end up in the emergency room today.*

Once I got in my car, my imagination was flooded with images of aggressive students and injured staff. The drive was not long enough for me to clear my mind, but I did the best I could to keep those thoughts at bay. When I arrived, I looked around the parking lot before getting out of my car. I didn't see anything out of the ordinary to give me additional pause, so I slowly walked toward the school trying to maintain perspective. Maybe, there was nothing to see, so I tried not to get ahead of myself.

As I reached the front door I could feel the tension in the air. It sat heavy in the entryway, a kind of static electricity on everyone's skin. My heart rate picked up. My body registered the threat that my mind had already anticipated.

Through the locked glass doors leading to the main part of the building, I could see the hallway crowded with students. There was a low roar of movement and chatter.

I paused for a second, took a deep breath, and thought, *You can't help anyone if you don't know what's really going on. You don't want to be the person safely tucked in a downtown office while your colleagues and friends are in danger.*

As the thumping in my chest began to fade, just a smidge, I firmly said to myself, *Put your big girl pants on and get your ass in there,* swiped my badge at the double glass doors, and stepped into the chaos.

As soon as I crossed the threshold, I heard someone screaming from far down the hallway. Two assistant principals ran past me, walkie-talkies blaring: "Assistance needed in the red cafeteria!"

I ducked and dodged my way around clusters of students and ran down the stairs after them.

When I reached the cafeteria, the two assistant principals were pushing their way into a tightly packed circle of teenagers. The students were cheering, shouting, and holding up their phones, videotaping an altercation I couldn't clearly see.

It was the first time in my work in schools that I felt truly unsafe.

What struck me just as much as the fight itself was the crowd's reaction. They weren't horrified. They were entertained. They had numeric proof of it in their phones: likes, comments, views.

I was also struck by the bravery—or maybe the sheer grit—of the assistant principals. They dove into that crowd without hesitation, putting their bodies between students who, in that moment, didn't seem to care if they got hurt themselves or hurt anyone else.

Feeling more like an observer than a supervisor, I ran back upstairs to recruit more help.

I never made it to the office.

"Walk with Me"

In the hallway, I ran into one of my former students from my elementary school days. I smiled a quick hello, grateful to see a familiar face.

Before he could respond, another student walked up and shoved him hard. My eyes widened. He was shoulder to shoulder with an adult—me—and the student pushed him anyway.

Within seconds, a crowd formed around us.

"You gonna let him do that to you?" one student shouted.
"Come on, you can't let that go!"
"What are you gonna do?"

I knew if I didn't intervene, this could escalate into another mob scene like the one I had just left downstairs.

There were no other adults nearby. I didn't have a walkie. It was an "every person for themselves" kind of moment.

I locked eyes with my former student.

"Walk with me," I said calmly, keeping my voice low enough that it cut under the noise instead of competing with it. "I know you can walk away from this with me."

I could hear the crowd still chirping in his ears.

"Oh, come on, you gonna let him get away with that?"
"You're a punk if you walk away."

For a second, I saw the indecision in his eyes. Then he made a choice.

He held my gaze and stepped away from the crowd with me.

We walked down the hall together while one by one students peeled off in search of other entertainment.

It was the one glimmer of hope that the kids were not out of reach yet.

I wish I could tell you that the rest of the year got easier after that. It didn't.

That first full year back after COVID was the most challenging year I have ever seen for school districts trying to maintain physical safety inside their buildings. It took the entire year for things to settle even a little.

The year after that was better relative to year one, but "better" is a relative term. Students still had enormous difficulty self-regulating.

The Two Sides of Social Isolation

The following year, each time I went into the school, I seemed to arrive during passing time, so I got a pretty consistent snapshot of hallway life, and what I saw was two distinct groups of students.

One group moved like ghosts: eyes glued to their phones, shoulders hunched, earbuds in. They weaved through the hallway without looking up, bumping into each other and into adults, barely registering anyone else's existence. They didn't speak to one another. Their attention lived in whatever was on their screen, completely socially isolated from the sea of people around them.

The other group moved like sparks: clusters of students fully engaged with each other, animated, loud, often profane. In those groups, it seemed like every third word was "motherf—er." Security guards tried to herd them along, urging them back to class while they lingered in packs, reluctant to go anywhere quiet. You could tell they were still rebounding from the year of COVID social isolation. There were no consequences or incentives that trumped what they craved most; face to face time with their peers. How could we blame them for seeking out those connections when peer relations are what matter most to teens?

In classrooms, I saw students asleep at their desks in the middle of the day, heads down, hoodies up, dark circles under their eyes. Counselors reported increasing numbers of students experiencing intense feelings of anxiety and depression.

Crisis evaluations for suicidal ideation went up. Absenteeism due to mental health concerns continued to rise.

On paper, we were talking about "anxiety," "depression," "behavioral issues," "school refusal." In my gut, I was seeing a generation of chronically sleep-deprived, overstimulated, under-supported kids who were trying desperately to function in a world that was not built for their nervous systems.

It was around this time that I went back to Matthew Walker's *Why We Sleep* with a highlighter and a notebook.

The Sleep Challenge

I had already seen, in my own body, what stable sleep could do. I had seen it in individual students—Teddy, the crying first grader, others who transformed with a simple nap or an earlier bedtime.

Now I wanted to see what would happen if we took this idea and applied it to a larger number of students.

In January 2022, I decided to create a district-wide "sleep challenge" which included a series of short videos used to educate students and staff about sleep.

With the help of local cable access, we produced a main video about the overall importance of sleep and a series of one to two-minute clips, each focused on a single strategy: keeping a consistent bedtime, keeping phones out of the bedroom, and so on. In each video I used a Judy Willis strategy to pique curiosity and increase engagement. The strategy is outlined in more detail in the chapter for educators, but to give you an idea here, each video starts out with a brain teaser and then provides the answer in the main part of the video.

I piloted the challenge with staff at a middle school before we ran it with students.

The structure was simple:

- Before the challenge, participants took a brief survey about their sleep habits, happiness and stress levels.
- On Monday, they watched the main video about sleep and its benefits.
- Each day for the next ten days, they watched one short video explaining the "why" behind a specific sleep strategy.
- Each morning, they filled out a quick form logging how many hours they slept the night before, which strategy they tried, and which one they planned to try that night.

The videos were strategically presented on specific days during the two-week timeframe to address things like irregular sleep schedules on the weekends and the overuse of caffeine to compensate for lost sleep.

It was not a perfect randomized controlled trial. It was a practical, real-world experiment inside a busy school.

The results were still sobering.

The bad news:

- Ninety-seven percent of students reported getting less than the recommended nine hours of sleep for their age group.
- Sixty percent reported getting six hours or less of sleep per night.

And remember: what they were actually reporting was time in bed, not time asleep. Even the best sleepers are only asleep about 85 percent of the time they're in bed. So, a student reporting six hours in bed might actually be getting closer to five hours and change of real sleep.

Either way, six hours or less is considered clinically significant sleep deprivation. At that level, mental health symptoms are more likely to emerge.

The good news:

Students who genuinely tried to implement the sleep strategies and increased their hours of sleep reported feeling better.

Their self-reported stress went down. Their mood improved. Many said they felt calmer, more focused, and more able to manage their emotions. The more effort they put into the challenge, the more benefit they reported.

It wasn't a magic cure. It didn't fix trauma or poverty or family systems. But it did make a noticeable difference.

Seeing those numbers—alongside the transformations I'd already seen in individual kids—left me both alarmed and hopeful.

On the one hand, the extent of sleep deprivation was frightening. On the other, the path to improvement was clearer than many of our more complicated interventions.

So, naturally, I thought, *Okay. This is it. We can end the youth mental health crisis if we just get kids sleeping better.*

I started speaking at schools and organizations. I wrote blog posts about sleep for Psychology Today. I talked about how better sleep could improve academic performance by up to 40 percent, increase emotional regulation, and reduce cravings for other riskier behaviors.

In my mind, it was a no-brainer.

Then I started speaking directly to youth in large groups.

That's when I realized: the science can be clear, the data can be compelling, the interventions can be simple—and it can still be very, very hard to change behavior in a world that is wired against it.

"I Can't Live Without My Phone"

I remember one youth summit in particular.

I was scheduled to be the second speaker that morning. I arrived a little early so I could get a feel for the room and mentally prepare.

As I walked into the auditorium, I saw a man on stage pouring his heart out about his battle with substance misuse. He talked about the consequences, the losses, the work it took to get sober. It was raw and vulnerable and, in my mind, exactly the kind of talk that should have had teenagers sitting at the edge of their seats.

That's not what was happening.

At least half of the students in the auditorium were asleep.

Not the polite, "I'm listening but my eyelids are heavy" kind of sleep. These kids were slumped down in their chairs, heads thrown back, legs sprawled out. Some had hats or hoods pulled over their faces. There was no attempt to hide it.

I stood in the back and thought, *I have never seen anything like this. Certainly not when I was in high school in the late '70s and early '80s.*

When it was my turn to speak, I faced a choice: talk to the students who were awake and ignore the sleeping ones, or try to wake everyone up and ask them to join us.

I chose the second option.

I took the microphone, walked up and down the aisles, and gently encouraged students to wake up, sit up, and join the conversation. I knew the kids who were asleep were the ones who needed to hear my talk.

I expected them to wake up groggy and maybe a little annoyed. I thought it might take a few minutes to get their attention but that, ultimately, it would be worth it.

That's not how it went.

Within moments, it was as if a bomb went off in the auditorium.

One student yelled at another to shut the f… up. That turned into pushing and yelling. A pocket of chaos exploded in the back of the room. There were more support staff in that auditorium than I'd seen at most events, which you'd think would deter that kind of behavior. It didn't.

It took a full-court press from adults to settle things enough for me to speak at all. Even then, the energy never fully calmed. Between the sleepiness, the distractions, and me being thrown off my game, I knew I didn't reach many of them that day.

At one point in the talk, I mentioned one of the most powerful (and most difficult) strategies for improving sleep was to put your phones outside of the bedroom at night.

A student shouted from the audience, "I can't live without my phone!"

He wasn't being cute. He meant it.

As part of the sleep challenge, I had asked students at the end which strategies they had not even attempted because they felt too difficult to do. The number one strategy they refused to try was putting electronics outside the bedroom. Number two was staying off social media.

The more I talked directly with youth, the clearer it became: they were not being dramatic when they said they "couldn't live" without their devices.

Their brains and nervous systems had adapted to constant stimulation and instant access and it was too uncomfortable for them to be without them.

Expecting them to simply "choose" better sleep without any structural support from adults was like asking someone to walk away from an open bar in the middle of a party when they'd never learned what alcohol does to their body.

They needed help.

What Sleep Showed Me

By this point in my journey, several things had become painfully clear:

- We have a generation of children and adolescents who are profoundly sleep-deprived.
- That sleep deprivation is being driven, in large part, by unregulated overuse of technology—especially at night.
- When we restore sleep, even slightly, kids feel better. They behave better. They learn better.
- **They cannot do this alone.**

I still believe that if we could get kids sleeping well again, we would see a drastic reduction in the number of students who need intensive mental health services. We would return to treating the historically vulnerable subset of youth who have always struggled, instead of trying to treat an entire generation.

But I also know this: adults have to go first.

Parents, caregivers, educators, leaders, and legislators need at least a basic understanding of:

- How sleep works.
- How technology affects the brain and body.
- How our current systems unintentionally undermine both.

Without that understanding, and without structural changes in homes, schools, and policy, we will continue to ask children to self-regulate in an environment that is almost perfectly designed to dysregulate them. This is where we'll go next.

Part 2

Chapter 4
Dopamine, Digital Life & Why Kids Feel Bad

When people talk about the youth mental health crisis, they often point to familiar culprits: trauma, poverty, domestic violence, substance use, unstable housing, or even the pandemic. These are serious drivers of distress, and they absolutely matter. But they are not new. Humanity has lived through wars, depressions, epidemics, and violence before without seeing this exact pattern of struggles in children and teens.

What feels different now is the environment—especially the digital environment our kids are growing up in.

Screens, social media, gaming platforms, online pornography, and 24/7 connectivity have entered almost every home on the planet. They shape how children play, socialize, fight, cope, and fall asleep (or don't). This environment is not neutral. It is interacting with a core part of our biology: dopamine, the brain chemical that drives motivation, reward, and "get up and go."

To understand why so many kids feel anxious, depressed, unfocused, and "fried," we first have to understand two things:

1. The basic hierarchy of human health, and
2. How the digital world hijacks dopamine in ways that make ordinary life feel unbearable by comparison.

These two forces—biology and environment—are colliding. And our kids' brains and bodies are stuck in the middle.

The Health Hierarchy: What the Body Needs First

When I step back and look at what truly moves the needle for health and resilience, I keep coming back to a simple, biologically grounded hierarchy. The components within the hierarchy are well-known to anyone interested in health, but how I arrange these components may be new to some of you. But bear with me. My reasoning is grounded in common sense, and cuts through the noise about healthy habits. Plus, there is plenty of science to back it up.

We are all individuals, but our bodies run on the same basic operating system. Certain inputs are more urgently needed than others. If we remove them, the body fails in a predictable order.

That order has shaped how I think about both prevention and healing, and it forms one of the core frameworks for this book.

The top five components of the health hierarchy are ranked as follows:

1. **Oxygen** (exercise and movement)
2. **Hydration**
3. **Sleep**
4. **Food and nutrition**
5. **Social connection**

This is not just a nice list of "healthy habits." The hierarchy is in the order of biological priority.

- Cut off **oxygen**, and a person will die in minutes. [6]
- Remove **water**, and survival is measured in days.[7]
- Remove **sleep**, and while we do not have definitive human experiments for ethical reasons, animal research and extreme human cases suggest that complete sleep deprivation is survivable only for a short window—likely days to a couple of weeks at most.[8]
- We can go the longest without **food**—around a month or more for many people.[9]
- And while you can't put an exact expiration date on loneliness, a lack of **social connection** steadily wears on the brain and body, driving chronic stress and disease.[10]

The closer something is to the top of this list, the faster the body and mind begin to fall apart when it is missing or disrupted. On the flip side, I would argue that interventions at the top of the hierarchy will positively impact the body more quickly than interventions at the bottom of the hierarchy. That said, the tier most impacted by a stressor should be the one prioritized for intervention. Either way, the hierarchy gives us a roadmap for where to focus our energy—especially when we're trying to help children and adolescents who are already overwhelmed.

---

1. Oxygen: Exercise and Movement

Oxygen utilization leads the charge because optimizing oxygen through movement, exercise, and even breathwork has a powerful impact on overall system performance. When we move our bodies—especially in ways that challenge the heart and lungs—we improve VO_2 max, the body's ability to use oxygen efficiently. Oxygen is not just about "fitness." It is fuel for every cell, including the brain. According to Mandsager et. al (2018) and many longevity specialists, it is also the number one indicator for longevity. [11]

For children, movement directly affects:

- **Mental health.** Physical activity helps regulate mood, reduce anxiety, and discharge stress hormones that would otherwise simmer in the system.
- **Learning.** Better oxygenation supports attention, working memory, and the ability to process information.
- **Stress recovery.** Movement is one of the most effective ways to metabolize cortisol and bring the nervous system back toward balance.

We cannot simply tell kids to "get off their phones" or "spend less time online" and expect compliance. We must offer compelling replacement activities—things that feel good, are socially rewarding, and give their bodies what their brains are craving at a deeper level. That means adults must intentionally build in more opportunities for play, movement, sports, dance, creative activities, and even simple walking—at home, in schools, and in communities. Adding these activities back in is one of the fastest ways to support kids.

2. Hydration: The Body's Transport System

Next comes hydration. Without water, a person can only survive a matter of days. Water is the transport medium for everything: nutrients, hormones, waste products, and electrolytes.

I think of hydration as the road system of the body. You can have the best nutrients and supplements in the world, but if there isn't enough properly mineralized water to carry them to their destination, the system underperforms.

Even mild dehydration in kids can lead to:

- Headaches
- Fatigue
- Irritability
- Difficulty concentrating [12]

Something as simple as making clean, appealing, mineral-rich water easily available to kids—who are often choosing soda, juice, or nothing at all—can have a profound impact on how they feel and function throughout the day.

3. Sleep: The Silent Reset (and Why We Come Back to It)

Sleep technically occupies the third spot in the health hierarchy, but in modern life it is often the most disrupted. One could argue that kids move less than they used to, and this is true, but the scale and consistency of sleep loss across age levels is staggering.

We'll devote the next chapter to sleep, because even though it sits in the third spot on the health hierarchy, it is the tier most impacted by technology, and since quality sleep is critical for emotional regulation, I am flagging sleep as the primary tier for intervention. It's that important. In fact, when I work with youth (and adults), **sleep restoration is the primary goal of treatment**. Why you may ask? I will go into this in more detail in the next chapter, but for now, suffice it to say that if you do not restore sleep, you are trying to correct a system that is fundamentally compromised, and any other interventions you try will be less effective. Interventions in a poorly slept body is like trying to operate a school with insufficient resources for the students, limited staff, and no lunch, bathroom or bussing schedule in place. You might hobble through the day, but you will never reach a full sprint.

4. Food and Nutrition: Fuel and Information

Because the body can survive weeks without food, nutrition appears fourth in the health hierarchy. But its importance for day-to-day functioning is enormous.

Food is not just fuel; it is information. It tells the body whether to:

- Build or break down tissue
- inflame or calm
- Stabilize or destabilize energy and mood

Children's brains and bodies are constantly building—neurons, synapses, muscle, and bone. When we give them nutrient-dense foods, adequate protein, healthy fats, and a variety of micronutrients, we support stable energy, mood, and focus. When their diets are dominated by ultra-processed foods, sugar spikes and crashes become the emotional backdrop of their day, making it much harder to self-regulate and learn.

Ultra-processed foods and drinks also often travel in the same spaces as screens: sipping sugary drinks while gaming, snacking on junk food while scrolling, using caffeine and energy drinks to stay awake for "just one more" level or show. Nutrition and digital habits become intertwined in ways that amplify stress on the brain.

5. Social Connection: The Antidote to Stress

The fifth tier on the health hierarchy is social connection, and I include it because of its powerful role in stress management. Oxytocin, often called the "bonding hormone," in certain contexts is released through warm, safe human contact and positive relationships. It can directly counteract the effects of cortisol, our primary stress hormone.[13]

For children, feeling seen, safe, and connected—at home, in school, and in the community—is not a luxury. It is part of their stress-management system. Genuine friendships, supportive adults, and inclusive communities help buffer them against the chronic pressures of modern life, including academic demands, social media stress, and family challenges.

The tragedy is that many children are more "connected" than ever online while feeling deeply disconnected in real life. Their cortisol remains elevated, while the social connections that could soothe it are in short supply because our communities have still not fully reconnected since the pandemic. Just look around you the next time you are on public transportation or even on an elevator. People don't make small talk with each other anymore. In fact, I was on a train in Boston heading up to Harvard one day, and even though there were at least 50 people in that car with me, not one person was talking and every single person on that car, including the kids, had their eyes glued to a phone. I can't imagine growing up as a young child now and wiring this type of scenario into my nervous system as the "way to show up in the world." This is so sad to me, but I digress.

The Body as a Masterpiece

Underneath this hierarchical framework is a core belief that guides my work: **the body is a masterpiece designed to heal and adapt when given the appropriate support**. Often, our job as adults is to supply those supports and then get out of the way.

Most parents, educators, and professionals are doing the best they can with the information and resources they have. I do not see a crisis of caring; I see a crisis of conditions. We have built environments—digital, educational, and social—that constantly activate children's stress systems while starving them of the very things that help them recover.

If we can:

- Reduce unnecessary stressors
- Increase opportunities for movement
- Provide clean, mineral-rich water
- Protect sufficient sleep
- Create environments rich in genuine connection

then many children's bodies and brains will begin to shift on their own. Cortisol levels can come down. Nervous systems can settle. Learning and emotional resilience can start to emerge more naturally.

The overall theme of this idea is simple but radical: when we design the environment well, children are far more likely to thrive. Our task is not to "fix" kids, but to reshape the systems around them so their remarkable capacity for healing, growth, and adaptation has a fair chance to do its work.

To understand how urgently that reshaping is needed, we have to zoom in on one particular system that the digital world targets over and over: **dopamine**.

What Is Dopamine Anyway?

Dopamine is a neurotransmitter that plays a central role in:

- Motivation and drive
- Goal-setting and persistence
- Movement and energy
- Anticipation of reward - "looking forward to something"

There's a famous experiment done in 1989 that I first heard about in a podcast that helps illustrate how critical dopamine is for survival. [14] In the experiment, scientists chemically removed the dopamine neurons in rats. When food was placed directly in their mouths, they chewed and swallowed it. But when food was placed just one body length away, the rats did not move to get it. They literally lacked the motivational spark to take that one small step.

Humans aren't rats, but the principle holds: without dopamine, we don't get up, seek, try, or care. Is this statement an oversimplification of how our highly complex brains function? Yes, but the point here is to provide a basic level of insight and understanding for the lay person.

In a healthy system, dopamine rises when:

- We anticipate something good (a meal, a game, a trip, a party).
- We take the steps needed to get there (cooking, practicing, planning, studying).
- We finally reach the goal (eating the meal, playing in the game, going to the party, finishing the project).

Dopamine is designed to be linked to effort over time. We evolved to work for our rewards: walking to get water, hunting or gathering food, preparing it, planning events, slowly building relationships. As we move through these steps, dopamine rises gradually, peaks when we reach the goal, and then gently settles back to baseline—what scientists call homeostasis.

That rhythm—anticipation, effort, reward, return to baseline—is part of what keeps our mood, focus, and motivation stable.

How the Digital Environment Hijacks Dopamine

Now consider what happens in our current digital environment:

- A child can access intense sexual content or pornography in seconds.
- Social media feeds deliver an endless stream of novelty, likes, and emotional drama.
- Short-form videos (reels, shorts, clips) are edited for maximum quick impact.
- Games are designed to keep users clicking, leveling up, and striving for the next hit.
- High-sugar foods, caffeine, and energy drinks are everywhere, often consumed alongside screens.

Each of these experiences triggers a rapid, high-intensity spike in dopamine. Instead of a gentle hill as we work toward a reward, the brain gets a sharp peak.

And what goes up that fast comes down just as fast. One could compare it to a blood sugar spike followed by a blood sugar crash from consuming foods high in sugar.

When we engage in activities that spike rather than gently raise dopamine, it creates a different response in the body. After a spike, dopamine levels don't just fall back to baseline; they dip below it, at least for a while. During that dip, kids (and adults) often feel:

- Flat or numb
- Bored and restless
- Irritable or anxious
- Down or depressed
- Driven to "just check" their phone, one more video, one more game

This is not a character flaw. It's physiology. The nervous system is trying to recalibrate after repeated peaks.

When this cycle of spike → crash → craving happens occasionally, the brain can recover. But when it happens dozens or hundreds of times a day—through scrolling, gaming, drama in group chats, rapid-fire videos, sugar, and caffeine—the brain starts to change in an effort to adapt to this type of environment.

Why "Normal Life" Feels Uncomfortable

Our brains are not static. They are constantly adjusting to the environment. When dopamine is pushed to high levels over and over, the brain essentially says:

> "This is too much. We need to turn the volume down."

One way it does this is by reducing the number or sensitivity of dopamine receptors. This process is often called neural adaptation.

The result is that:

- The old "normal" no longer feels good.
- Everyday activities—reading a book, sitting in class, talking with family—feel dull and empty.
- Kids may say, "I'm bored," "I hate this," or "Nothing is fun unless I'm online."
- It now takes more stimulation just to feel okay. They're not necessarily "chasing a high"—they're trying to climb out of that below-baseline dip.

Some people call this pattern addiction, but I prefer to refer to it as neural adaptation for two reasons. I find the term to be more compassionate and less stigmatizing. It also accurately describes a normal physiological response. The brain and the body were designed to adapt to new environments. So, in this case, the brain is doing what it is designed to do. The problem is not our brains, it is the extremes within our environment and the conditions we've created.

When kids (or adults) suddenly cut back on high-dopamine activities—like late-night gaming, constant scrolling, energy drinks, or pornography—they can experience a cluster of universal symptoms that include:

- Anxiety
- Irritability
- Agitation and restlessness
- Insomnia or difficulty winding down
- Low mood or depression
- Intense craving for "just a little bit more"

This is what many people call withdrawal. In everyday life, it often shows up as, "I feel awful when I'm not on my phone," or "I can't sleep without my show," or "I get really angry when I have to log off."

This is why willpower alone is often not enough. We are asking children—and ourselves—to fight biology in an environment that constantly pushes dopamine to the edge.

And nowhere does this show up more powerfully, and more dangerously, than in the way dopamine and screens collide with sleep.

In the next chapter, we'll look at how this collision plays out in real time in kids' bedrooms, classrooms, and nervous systems—and why repairing sleep may be one of the most powerful exit ramps we have out of the youth mental health crisis.

Chapter 5
Why Sleep Is a Foundation, Not a Luxury

When we talk about youth mental health, we often jump straight to diagnoses, therapy, or medication. What we talk about much less is **sleep**. Yet sleep is one of the most powerful—and most overlooked—drivers of emotional health, physical health, and school functioning.

In the health hierarchy, sleep comes after oxygen and water in terms of survival time. But in day-to-day life, it has become one of the **most compromised** tiers on the health hierarchy. Kids may still be breathing and drinking, but their sleep is collapsing under the weight of academic pressures, social lives, and the digital world.

It is also worth noting that sleep disruption, in one form or another, is a hallmark of many major mental health diagnoses. [15] That is why, in my work, **sleep restoration is step one**. When we help young people recover their sleep, everything else—mood, behavior, learning, even family relationships—has a better chance of improving.

Sleep Is Not "Doing Nothing"

Sleep is not "down time." It is one of the most active, busy times in the life of the brain and body. During the night, we cycle through different stages of sleep, each with its own job.

- **Deep, non-REM sleep** is when the body does much of its repair work. Cells are restored, tissues heal, and the immune system is strengthened.
- **REM sleep**, when most dreaming happens, is our emotional and creative "processing lab." The brain works through memories, problems, and feelings, trying to make sense of the day.

When children and teens don't get enough sleep, a lot of important work simply doesn't get done.

- **Physical repair suffers.** Damaged cells are not repaired as effectively, and injuries heal more slowly. Over time, chronic sleep loss contributes to wear and tear on the body.
- **The immune system is weakened.** With inadequate sleep, immune cells become less active and less efficient. Kids get sick more often and stay sick longer.
- **Learning and memory are impaired.** New information is "stored" and organized during sleep. Without that consolidation time, learning can drop dramatically. Some research suggests that significant sleep deprivation can reduce learning and academic performance by up to 40%.[16]
- **Stress and trauma are harder to process.** Challenging and traumatic experiences need to be "filed away" and integrated. When kids are sleeping well, they often wake up and say, "This doesn't feel quite as overwhelming as it did yesterday." When they're not, those memories and emotions stay raw and unprocessed.
- **Impulses and cravings become harder to manage.** Sleep deprivation makes it much harder to resist cravings for food, substances, or screens. The sleepy brain is more likely to reach for quick hits of pleasure and less able to pause and choose a healthier option.
- **Mood and emotional regulation suffer.** Tired brains are irritable, anxious, and reactive. This can look like depression, anxiety, "behavior problems," or "attitude," when underneath it all is a nervous system that simply hasn't rested.

When we look at many of the behaviors that worry adults—explosiveness, withdrawal, lack of motivation, poor focus—it is worth asking a simple question first: *How is this child sleeping?*

Sleep Opportunity vs. Sleep Reality

It's also important to understand that when we say a person "sleeps eight hours," we often mean they are in bed for eight hours. But no one sleeps solidly from the moment their head hits the pillow to the moment the alarm goes off. We all wake briefly throughout the night.

That has always been true, but it means that to get eight hours of actual sleep, a person needs more than eight hours of sleep opportunity—time in bed, in a dark, quiet environment, with the possibility of sleeping.

For many young people, that means they need significantly more time in bed than they are currently getting. Depending on age, that could mean:

- Earlier bedtimes
- Later school start times
- Or both

Without enough sleep opportunity, the math simply doesn't work. You can't squeeze ten hours of necessary sleep into six or seven hours of available time.

Circadian Rhythms: The Brain's Master Clock

All human bodies function best with a schedule. In fact, the body has a central clock located in the brain called the suprachiasmatic nucleus. This central clock is the body's master clock and governs the body's sleep-wake cycle. According to the Center for Chronobiology [17] all of the body's organs and glands also have clocks. Each organ is synchronized with the central clock and knows when to perform certain duties based on its connection to the master clock. The master clock works best when it is consistently exposed to light in the morning and darkness at night.

When a young person goes to bed and wakes up at roughly the same time every day, that clock can do its job:

- **Cortisol** rises in the morning to wake the body up.
- **Melatonin** rises in the evening to prepare it for sleep.

How Digital Life Attacks Sleep

The modern digital environment makes all of this much harder. We now have a perfect storm of light, content, chemistry, and timing working against healthy sleep.

1. **Light exposure.**
   Bright screens in the evening and at night suppress melatonin, the hormone that signals to the body that it's time to sleep. A teen who is on a bright screen right up until bedtime may not even feel sleepy at a healthy hour because their brain hasn't been allowed to turn on the sleep signal.
2. **Overstimulation and emotional intensity.**
   Fast, emotionally loaded digital content ramps up the nervous system. Right before bed, many young people are exposed to arguments in group chats, frightening news, intense gaming, or sexual content. Their brains are in fight-or-flight mode at the exact time when they need to be winding down.
3. **Dopamine peaks and crashes.**
   Remember the dopamine spikes we talked about in the previous chapter? Late at night, those spikes are especially disruptive. A child is not just losing hours of sleep; they are also training their brain to expect high stimulation at a time of day when it should be quieting down. When the device finally goes off, the brain is still buzzing—and for those whose dopamine systems have adapted to constant stimulation, nighttime can feel like withdrawal.
4. **Chemical stimulants.**
   Energy drinks, caffeinated sodas, vaping, and sugary snacks often accompany late-night digital use. These substances further confuse the body's signals about when it is time to sleep and when it is time to be awake.

Any students who are up gaming, scrolling, or chatting online between 1:00 a.m. and 5:00 a.m., are often doing so without the adults in their lives knowing. By the time morning comes, their cortisol and dopamine systems are completely out of sync with the school day in front of them.

When Sleep Loss Looks Like Mental Illness

Chronic sleep deprivation alone can mimic or worsen:

- Anxiety
- Depression

- Irritability and mood swings
- Difficulty concentrating and learning
- Hyperactivity and impulsivity

Sound familiar? These are many of the same symptoms that lead to diagnoses like anxiety disorders, mood disorders, and ADHD. And here is probably one of the most important things to know about sleep loss. **Sleep deprivation alone, in the absence of other stressors, can trigger thoughts of suicide and suicide attempts.** [18] Let that thought sink in for a moment.

This doesn't mean those diagnoses are never accurate or helpful. But if we ignore the combined impact of digital overstimulation, neural adaptation, and sleep loss, we risk misreading a large portion of the youth mental health crisis and end up medicating youth unnecessarily. We will keep treating symptoms in isolation, without changing the conditions that are flooding kids' brains and bodies every day.

Dopamine, Sleep, and the "Fried" Brain

If dopamine is the engine, sleep is the repair shop. And right now, many children (and adults) are trying to keep driving without ever pulling in for maintenance.

Here's the cycle I see over and over:

1. A child or teen is exposed to constant high-dopamine stimulation—games, social media, pornography, short-form videos, sugar, caffeine.
2. Their brain adapts by turning the dopamine "volume" down, so everyday life feels dull and uncomfortable.
3. To escape that discomfort, they seek more of the same stimulation, often late into the night.
4. This overstimulation and late-night light exposure wreck their sleep.
5. Sleep loss makes them more emotionally fragile, more impulsive, more stressed, and more desperate for quick relief.

6. The cycle repeats, often daily.

From the outside, this can look like defiance, laziness, or lack of caring. From the inside, it feels like being stuck in a loop you can't get out of. When a child says, "I can't sleep without my show," or "I get so mad when my phone is taken away," what we are often seeing is not just "attitude," but the combined weight of dopamine withdrawal and sleep deprivation.

Understanding this doesn't excuse harmful behavior, but it does change how we respond. It moves us from blame toward problem-solving.

Why Sleep Comes First in the Exit Plan

Every tier on the health hierarchy can have a positive impact on the other tiers. So, ideally, we could intervene on any one of the tiers and children's mental health will likely improve to some degree. That said, if we don't target the tier that is most compromised by the current conditions, reaching the ultimate goal of wellness is much less likely if not impossible. Since sleep deprivation is so widespread, if we are serious about exiting the youth mental health crisis, we have to be serious about sleep.

That means:

- **Designing homes, schools, and policies** that respect sleep as a biological necessity, not a negotiable privilege.
- **Creating technology boundaries** that protect our children's brains and the evening hours.
- **Helping kids and families** gently taper high-dopamine activities so their brains can recalibrate.
- **Building daily rhythms**—movement, hydration, nutrition, and connection—that support healthy sleep rather than fight against it.

When we start with sleep, we are not ignoring trauma, poverty, racism, bullying, or other very real sources of suffering. We are building the physiological foundation that allows children to have a fighting chance to cope with those realities.

In the chapters that follow, we will move from biology to blueprint. I'll lay out concrete "exit plans" for parents, educators, and legislators—specific, realistic steps to reshape the environments around children so that their sleep, dopamine systems, and overall health can begin to repair.

We will not be asking individual kids to somehow will their way out of a system that is stacked against them. Instead, we will be asking the adults—and the systems we control—to change the rules of the game.

Part 3

Chapter 6
Exit Plan for Parents

The Rock and the Hard Place

If you are a parent who picked up this book, you are likely looking for answers either for your own family or for someone you care about. You are the parent I am trying to reach because I believe you will be part of the solution I present in this book. So, let's get something clear up front. You are not a bad parent for ending up here. Let's start there.

You have been raising kids in an environment that did not exist when you were a child. You are trying to do your best in a world where the most powerful companies on the planet are competing for your child's attention 24/7, with tools specifically designed to bypass self-control. Of course, this feels hard. Of course, you sometimes feel like you're losing.

When I talk publicly about changing laws to better protect children from exploitative technology, I sometimes hear, "It starts at home. Parents just need to take responsibility for what they allow their kids to do."

I want to be very clear with you: right now, our cultural norms have you firmly wedged between a rock and a very hard place.

All of our homes were flooded with technology with no warning labels included with them. And now that everyone has technology, it makes it very hard to be the only one to remove it. Most of us who are now adults remember exactly how painful it was to feel left out as teenagers. You know what it's like to be the only one not invited, the only one not wearing what everyone else is wearing, the only one not allowed to do what all your peers are doing. So of course, you hesitate to make your child "the only one" without a phone, a social media account, a gaming system, or late-night online access.

On top of that, it is completely understandable if you assume that the government would have stepped in years ago if online technology was truly as dangerous as some of us are now saying it is. That's how we handled car seats, lead paint, tobacco, and toys with choking hazards. It is reasonable to think, "If it were really that bad, someone would have done something by now."

Meanwhile, as someone who has worked for decades in schools, counseling children and teens, I have watched many very competent, very involved parents get blindsided by the consequences of their child's digital life. Not because they are careless or don't care, but because this environment is designed to be invisible to you.

Based on my work with kids, I learned that many kids continue their online activity when you are asleep. In the sleep challenge data I collected, this was a consistent theme. **Many youths reported going back online after "bedtime"** and staying on devices well into the night, often in secret. Dr. Elizabeth Englander's work through the Massachusetts Aggression Reduction Center (MARC) has reported similar patterns in youth digital behavior. [19] This means your child may be:

- Engaging online while severely overtired
- Making decisions with an underdeveloped frontal lobe (the part of the brain that manages judgment and impulse control)
- Completely unsupervised, even though they are technically "at home"

That combination—exhausted, unsupervised, and connected to the entire world—is a setup for engaging in risky behaviors that lead to devastating consequences.

It also makes it much harder for your child or teen to reach out for help if something goes wrong. If they've violated a family rule ("No phone after bedtime") or at least an expectation you thought was understood, they may feel ashamed, afraid of punishment, or terrified you'll overreact. So, they stay silent and try to manage situations that are too big for them: harassment, sextortion, exposure to self-harm content, sexual advances from adults, or social exclusion.

To make this more complicated, many teens simply don't want to talk to their parents about their problems—especially the ones that feel the most painful. In my counseling work, I have heard so many reasons:

"I don't want to disappoint them."
"I don't want to worry them."
"They'll just take my phone away."
"They'll tell me to ignore it; they won't get it."
"If I tell them, they'll freak out or call the school and make it worse."

This is not a criticism of you. This is exactly why school counselors, therapists, and other trusted adults exist: to help kids navigate problems that feel too big to bring directly to their parents, and to support them in getting help when a parent really does need to be brought into the fold.

I'm telling you all of this so that as we move into a practical "exit plan" for you and your family, you can let go of guilt and blame. You have been swimming upstream in a very fast river. You did not create this river—but you and your child still have to get to shore together.

The plan that follows is focused on what you can do at home right now, because we cannot wait until the laws change. The stakes are too high to wait for legislative action, when you can start using the tools presented next, to protect your family now. I will talk directly to you, as one adult to another. You know your child best. You know your family's culture, stressors, and strengths. Take what fits, adjust what needs adjusting, and leave the rest.

Before You Try to Change Your Child, Start with You

Before I ask you to change anything about your child's behavior, I'm going to ask you to take an honest look at your own habits and the expectations in your home.

This is not about shaming you. It's about setting you up for success.

Kids learn best by watching adults model healthy behaviors. So, if you ask your child to put away their phone while you are still scrolling in bed, or to get off the game while your own laptop is open, you are fighting an uphill battle. So, step one in this exit plan is an internal inventory.

You might literally grab a notebook or your phone and ask yourself:

Do we have clear expectations in this house around technology, sleep, and daily routines, or are things more vague and "unspoken"?
Have I provided the structure, support, and guidance my child needs to be successful with those expectations?
Am I consistently modeling the behavior I expect? (For example, do I put my own phone away at night? Do I prioritize my own sleep?)
When I am exhausted or stressed, do I rely on screens to "babysit" my child because I'm overwhelmed? (No judgment here—this is very common.)

If your habits are mostly aligned with what you want for your child, you are in a strong position to move ahead.

If you notice gaps—welcome to the human race. I would simply encourage you to make changes in your own behavior either before or at the same time that you ask your child to change theirs. That shared effort will go a long way toward lowering defensiveness and building trust.

The Parent Exit Plan: Eight Practical Steps

I'm going to walk you through eight core steps you can start using now. You do not have to do them all at once. In fact, I don't recommend that. Start at the beginning and work your way through the steps. You may be in a great place in some areas and be able to skip steps that you already have in place. Consider dedicating more time and energy on steps that address the biggest pain points for your family and gradually expand.

Step 1: Start with an Honest, Compassionate Inventory (You and Your Household)

You've already begun this step by reading the questions above, but let's make it more concrete.

Think about the following areas:

Sleep in your home
What time does your child actually fall asleep most nights?
What time do they actually wake up?
Do they seem rested, or are mornings a daily battle?

Technology locations and routines
Where do phones, tablets, computers, and gaming consoles live at night?
Are devices allowed at the table, in the car, in bedrooms?
Do you have any explicit family rules written down?

Your own habits
Do you sleep with your phone next to you?
Do you check email "one last time" at midnight?
Do you watch TV or scroll to fall asleep?

You are not grading yourself; you are gathering information.

If you notice that your own habits are not where you want them to be, consider choosing one small change for yourself that mirrors what you plan to ask of your child. For example:

If you want your child's phone out of the bedroom at night, move your own charging station to the kitchen too.
If you want your child to get to bed earlier, commit to your own regular bedtime and talk openly about why.

Kids are much more likely to respect boundaries that they see you honoring as well.

Step 2: Have a Calm, Collaborative Talk with Your Child

Once you've taken your own inventory, the next step is to talk with your child or teen about your concerns and your hopes. The goal here is connection and collaboration, not laying down the law.

Pick a time when:

No one is rushing out the door.
You are not already in conflict about technology.
You have at least 20–30 minutes to talk without constant interruptions.

You might start with something like:

"I've been learning more about how technology affects sleep and overall health. I'm realizing that the way things are set up right now may not be great for any of us—including me. I'm concerned about how much pressure you're under, how late you're up, and how hard it is to unplug. I don't want to punish you. I want us to figure out together how to make this healthier and less stressful."

Then invite your child in:

"What are your thoughts when you hear my concerns? What feels hard or scary about making changes? What do you already wish were different?"

And then: let them talk.

As they share concerns, resist the urge to jump in with counter-arguments. Instead, reflect back what you hear so they know you are listening:

"I hear you saying that if we change your sleep and tech habits, you're worried you won't have enough time to talk with friends."
"It sounds like you're afraid you'll be out of the loop if you're not online late at night."
"You're worried your homework will pile up if you don't stay up late to finish it."

Your goal in this step is not to solve everything. It's to show your child: I am on your side. I care about what matters to you. We will solve this together.

Step 3: Build a Collaborative Plan to Address Both Concerns

Once your child feels heard, you can move into what psychologist Dr. Ross Greene calls a "collaborative and proactive solutions" approach.[20]

In simple terms, this means:

Your concern goes on the table (for example, lack of sleep, exposure to harmful content, or declining grades).
Your child's concern goes on the table (for example, losing connection with

friends, or feeling behind in a game or online community).
Then you work with your child to come up with a plan that **addresses both sets of concerns** as much as possible.

You might say:

"I want to make sure you have enough time to connect with friends and get the sleep your brain needs. Let's brainstorm ways to do both. What are some options we could try?"

Together, you might come up with ideas like:

Moving friend-chat time to earlier in the evening.
Having a nightly "check-in" where they can show you funny memes or updates before devices get turned in.
Setting a firm tech cutoff time on school nights, with a slightly later one on weekends.
Creating a short, protected block of time after dinner that is just for homework, so they are less likely to be doing it at midnight.

As you brainstorm, you can gently bring your own non-negotiable concerns into the conversation:

"One thing I'm not willing to compromise on is that you need enough sleep to function and stay healthy. The science is really clear on that. So whatever plan we come up with, it has to protect your sleep. Within that boundary, I'm very open to getting creative."

When you involve your child in planning in this way, you shift from "I'm doing this to you" to "We're doing this together." That shift alone often reduces power struggles.

At this point, you may feel tempted to start with the easiest changes. But for most families, the biggest immediate impact comes from protecting the night—because sleep affects everything else.

Step 4: Protect the Night and the Bedroom

Now we move into a step that many families find difficult—but that is powerful enough to change everything: removing electronics from bedrooms at night.

I consider this **my top recommendation to parents**, regardless of your child's age.

No internet-connected devices in bedrooms overnight means no smartphones, tablets, laptops, gaming systems, or TVs. If you find you have too many electronics throughout your home to move them all to one location, you can approach this idea in one of two ways. If you only have smartphones to deal with, the easiest approach is to create a central charging station in a common area—kitchen, hallway, living room—and make "plugging in" part of the bedtime routine for everyone, including you. If there are several devices in each room, the other approach could be to cut off internet connection to all internet connected devices at a certain time each night.

This step alone will help reduce the opportunities for kids to engage in:

Risky challenges ("just try this once…")
Aggressive or sexually explicit messages
Requests to send images
Online bullying or exclusion
Content that feeds self-harm, eating disorders, or hopelessness

Since most children and teens do not yet have the brain maturity to self-manage their online time, **they need you to step in and provide structure**. If your child or teen raises a fuss about this step, it is a pretty clear indicator that they need your help.

If your child is behaviorally challenged or easily dysregulated, offering choices within the non-negotiables can help. For example:

"We've decided that devices will not be operational in bedrooms at night anymore. That part is not up for debate—it's about safety and health, but you can choose between the following two options:
– to permanently use and store all your devices in the living room (or other common area), or

– to keep your devices in your room during the day and bring them into the common area before bed each night.
Which would you rather do?"

This strategy is very commonly used as a go-to strategy for staff working in programs that serve behaviorally challenged youth and can be very effective when done correctly.

Whatever you choose, the key is to follow through consistently. Inconsistency invites arguments and repeated arguments results in exhaustion on your part and ultimately a breakdown in the system you wish to maintain. Clear, steady limits—paired with warmth and explanation—help kids feel both safe and respected because they know you care enough to follow through.

This step also sets you up perfectly for the next part of the chapter, where we'll go even deeper into sleep. But before we get there, it helps to build some replacement activities and daily rhythms so the change doesn't just feel like a loss.

Step 5: Add Replacement Activities and Daily Rhythms to Support Sleep

You cannot pull something big out of a child's life—like late-night gaming, endless scrolling, or constant texting—without putting something in its place. Otherwise, the hole left behind will be filled by more of the same behavior, just at another time or through another device.

So, as you are talking about sleep and technology, start thinking in terms of replacement activities and daily rhythms that support healthy sleep and a calmer nervous system.

Ask yourself:

How much physical activity does my child get most days?
Do they spend any time outside, especially in the morning or afternoon light?
Do they have regular in-person social contact (teams, clubs, faith

communities, hobbies) that is not based on phones or gaming?
Do we have any kind of evening wind-down routine that signals to the body, "We're getting ready for sleep"?

Simple changes can make a big difference:

Encouraging your child to walk or bike instead of driving when possible.
Signing them up for an activity they choose and enjoy (sports, martial arts, theater, music, art, robotics, dance—anything that uses their body and brain in ways that feel good).
Building small family rituals: a nightly walk after dinner, a quick card game, reading together, or talking about "highs and lows" of the day.
Spending more time in natural light earlier in the day, which helps set the body's sleep-wake cycle.

These activities are not "extra." They are key pieces of helping your child's brain and body be ready for sleep at night—and they naturally reduce the time and energy available for endless screen use.

Step 6: Learn Your Child's Digital World

You cannot help your child navigate a world you have never seen.

One of the most powerful things you can do is to sit with your child or teen and ask them to show you what they do online.

Not to interrogate them. Not to spy. To learn.

You might say:

"I know you spend a lot of time online, and I realize there are apps and games I've never even heard of. Would you be willing to give me a tour of your digital world? I'm not here to judge what you are doing; I just want to understand what it's like for you."

Let them show you:

Which social media platforms they use
Which games they play
Which group chats or Discord servers they are in
Which influencers they follow
What a "normal" night online looks like

As you watch, gently ask curious questions:

"What do you like about this game?"
"How do people usually talk to each other in this chat?"
"What happens if someone is mean or crosses a line?"
"What would you do if someone asked you for a picture you didn't want to send?"

You are gathering information and quietly looking out for red flags, such as:

Adults interacting in kid spaces in ways that seem too personal
Communities that glorify self-harm, hatred, or extreme dieting
Games or chats where racist, sexist, or homophobic slurs are common and unchallenged
Pressure to send revealing photos or videos

If you see something that concerns you, you don't have to react in front of them at that moment. You can make a mental note, come back later for a calmer conversation, and, if needed, set new boundaries.

The more you understand your child's digital world, the better you can protect them and collaborate with them.

Step 7: Set Up Safety Nets, Passwords, Agreements, and Trusted Adults

Some of the most heartbreaking stories in this space come from parents who lost their children and then could not access their phones or accounts in time to understand what happened or to respond to threats.

Parents who have been through this often say the same thing to others: Make sure you have your child's passwords.

That does not mean you read every message every day. It means:

In an emergency, you can get in.
If something feels "off," you can look more closely.

You might say:

"As your parent, it's my job to keep you safe. That includes your online world. I don't want to hover over everything you do. But I do need to have your passwords in case of an emergency or if something truly dangerous is happening. I'm asking you to trust that I will use them responsibly, not as a way to humiliate or control you."

Consider reviewing a phone or device agreement together. There are some excellent templates online, including from organizations like Culture Reframed, that spell out: [21]

What devices are for
Where and when they can be used
What happens if rules are broken
What you commit to as a parent (for example, not reading every message unless there is a safety concern)

Equally important is to have a harm-reduction conversation with your child or teen:

"If you ever get in trouble online—if you send something you regret, if someone threatens you, if you see something that scares or confuses you—I want you to know you can come to me. My first response will not be to yell or immediately take everything away. My first focus will be on keeping you safe and helping you figure out what to do next.

If for some reason you feel like you can't talk to me, I want you to promise me you'll talk to another trusted adult—maybe a school counselor, teacher, coach, or another family member. You do not have to handle it alone."

You cannot guarantee that your child will always come to you first. But you can make it as emotionally safe as possible for them to do so, and you can give explicit permission for them to reach out to other adults if that feels easier for them.

Step 8: Consider the Ultimate Gift

The greatest gift you can give your child/teen is the gift of a dopamine fast. What does this look like? It would involve removing all devices for a period of 1-2 weeks. This might seem like an impossibility for many reasons, but if you can swing it, I would highly recommend it. The fast would allow your child to experience what life is like when the body has reached its true baseline.

Even if after the fast your child/teen goes right back to heavily using technology, they will at least have a reference point for what life could feel like if they weren't constantly stimulated. It will help them appreciate the simpler things in life, and that alone can increase feelings of wellbeing.

If you want to try something like this, I would recommend trying it during a school vacation or summer break. You will want to make sure your child/teen has plenty of outdoor movement activities available to them so their bodies have an outlet for the excess agitation they will feel during the process. An ideal place to do something like this would be at a campsite where there are plenty of outdoor activities around.

Be prepared for a solid 2 days of "This is awful! I hate this! I hate you for making me do this! I can't live like this." If you have arranged for them to be busy enough during that time period, it should start to get better from there. If your child or teen's nervous system has been totally hijacked, it may take up to a couple of weeks without high level stimulation before they start feeling better. Giving kids the opportunity to experience life without overstimulation gives them a better chance of developing the self-awareness and self-regulation skills that allow them to effectively respond in ways that keep their body resilient to stress.

A Word of Caution Before You Remove Devices:

If you are reading this and feel like you want to run to your kid's room and remove all devices without taking the recommended steps outlined in this chapter, please don't. It is important to know that an abrupt or unannounced removal of devices can be so distressing to youth that it can land them in the emergency room. Device removal is now a common precipitant that can lead to a crisis evaluation. Rather than acting in haste, think of these changes as a gradual process. It is more of a marathon rather than a sprint. While the situation is clearly urgent, our response to it must be carefully executed if we want to help our kids in a way that demonstrates empathy and understanding.

Additional Consideration: Partner with the School if They Raise Concerns

If the school reaches out to tell you they are worried about your child's behavior, attention, mood, or academic performance, it can be painful. You may feel embarrassed, defensive, or shocked—especially if your child seems very different at home.

I want you to know that it is very common for schools to see a side of a child that the family does not see, and vice versa. That doesn't mean the school is right about everything. It means they are seeing your child in a different environment, with different stressors and social dynamics.

Instead of assuming, "They're exaggerating" or "They are targeting my child," consider:

Asking for a meeting (in person or virtually) to understand the specifics of their concerns.
Requesting concrete examples: When is your child struggling most? What does it look like? What time of day?
Sharing what you see at home—sleep patterns, device use, mood, and any changes in behavior.

School staff may be able to help you see patterns like:

Falling asleep in class (a clear sign of sleep deprivation)
Increased irritability, conflicts with peers, or withdrawal
Difficulty concentrating or finishing work

Together, you and the school can come up with a shared plan. That might include:

Limiting screen time at home on school nights.
Scheduling screen time after homework instead of before school.
Removing screens in the morning before school to allow more time for getting ready and eating.
Providing alternative activities at home that support good sleep (quiet reading, relaxation routines, calming music).

You don't have to agree with every suggestion the school makes, but staying in conversation helps avoid a "home vs. school" dynamic. Ideally, your child should receive a clear, consistent message from both environments: We are on your side. We want you healthy, rested, and supported. When parents and schools work together, this is the best equation for student success.

At this point in the chapter, I want to pause and highlight a theme you may have already noticed:

No matter which angle we look from—behavior, mood, school performance, physical health—we keep coming back to sleep.

Sleep is not just one item on a checklist. It is the foundation under almost everything else.

You cannot fix every problem in your child's life by improving sleep, but you will make every other intervention more effective if sleep is protected.

That's why the final section of this chapter goes deeper into concrete, doable sleep strategies. Think of everything we've talked about so far—your own habits, collaborative planning, replacement activities, nighttime boundaries, digital literacy, safety nets, and school partnership—as the scaffolding. Now we'll focus on the foundation those beams rest on: your child's sleep.

Helping Your Child Reclaim Healthy Sleep

You have probably heard the message that "kids need more sleep" so many times that your eyes glaze over when someone says it again. The problem is that you are rarely given clear, realistic steps that fit your actual life—the one with late practices, homework, commuting, younger siblings, and jobs that don't always allow you to be home at 7:00 p.m. starting a peaceful bedtime routine.

I want to be very clear: the goal is not perfection.

The goal is to steadily move your child's sleep in a healthier direction.

You can think in terms of "better than before," not "perfect or nothing."

Here are core recommendations that make a meaningful difference for most families.

1. Aim for Enough Sleep Opportunity

When parents say, "Oh, they get eight hours of sleep," what they often mean is: my child is in bed for eight hours. But because we all wake up briefly during the night—sometimes without remembering it—eight hours in bed usually translates into closer to seven hours of actual sleep, sometimes less. The following is a general guideline by age level. You will need to adjust the hours based on your individual child's needs.

For elementary and middle school aged children, a realistic target is 9-13 hours of actual sleep. The younger the child the more sleep they will need. For teens, a realistic target is 8-10 hours of actual sleep.[22] This means you need to build in enough sleep opportunity (time in bed in a dark, quiet room) in order to get the number of hours of actual sleep their brains and bodies need. Keep in mind, really young children need even more sleep than what is noted here.

"Sleep opportunity" matters because it builds in time for the normal wake-ups that happen at night.

So, ask yourself:

What time does my child/teen actually need to wake up on school days? Working backward, what bedtime gives them at least 10+ hours in bed for children and at least 9+ hours in bed for teens.

For example, if your child must be up at 6:00 a.m.:

The ideal bedtime for adequate sleep opportunity would be somewhere between 6-8 p.m. depending on the age and individual needs of your child.

If your teen must be up at 6 am, the ideal bedtime to allow for adequate sleep would be 8-9 pm.

If your child/teen is regularly:

Up late on devices
Doing homework at midnight
Waking early for practices or activities

…they are almost certainly under slept, even if, on paper, it looks like they were "in bed" long enough.

You don't have to change the schedule overnight. Start by shifting bedtime 15–30 minutes earlier and holding that for a couple of weeks. Then shift again if needed.

2. Keep a Consistent Sleep and Wake Schedule

One of the most powerful (and underrated) things you can do is:

Set a regular wake time and stick to it, even on weekends, with only small adjustments. The regular schedule provides the type of structure and consistency the body needs to function at its best. Imagine a school trying to function without a schedule. One day the school opens at 8 am and another day it opens at 10 am. All the systems that keep schools running like clockwork when a consistent schedule is in place become dysfunctional; think bussing, academic support, lunch, recess, and after school activities. If the school opened at random times throughout the week, the whole system would be thrown into chaos. When we set a regular wake time, in particular, all the functions of the body are well-timed and predictable.

That might sound impossible if your teen is used to sleeping until noon on Saturdays after being up half the night. But sleeping in that late—even if it feels like "catching up"—actually confuses the central clock in the brain and makes Sunday night and Monday morning even harder. When bedtimes bounce between 9:30 p.m. on school nights and 2:00 a.m. on weekends, that clock never really stabilizes. The result is a body and brain that feel "off" much of the time: groggy in the morning, wired at night, and emotionally shaky in between.

For many students, their weekly schedule looks like traveling across multiple time zones every weekend and then trying to function in school on Monday as if nothing happened.

A more helpful pattern looks like:

A consistent wake time and bed time on school days.
On weekends, a wake time that is maybe 1 hour later with a 30-minute afternoon nap, not a 5–6 hours later wake time.

Once you pick a wake time, you then work backward to determine when lights need to be out to provide enough sleep opportunity.

Does this mean your teen will never sleep in again? No. There will be days after illness or intense weeks where a little extra morning sleep is reasonable. But as a general pattern, consistency beats extremes.

3. Build a Simple, Predictable Bedtime Routine

A bedtime routine does not have to be elaborate. It is simply a series of cues that tell the brain and body: We are getting ready for sleep now.

You might:

Start winding things down 60–90 minutes before bedtime.
Dim the lights in your home.
Encourage quieter activities: reading, drawing, gentle stretching, listening to calm music, or simply talking about the day.
Consider a warm shower or bath; as the body cools afterward, it naturally supports the onset of sleep.
Avoid intense homework, arguments, or emotionally heated conversations right before bed when possible.

Think of the routine as a rhythm you repeat most nights. It does not have to be exactly the same from day to day, but enough of it should be predictable that your child/teen's nervous system begins to recognize, "Oh, this is what we do before sleep."

If your evenings are chaotic—multiple kids, late work shifts, activities—aim for small anchor points. For example:

A consistent "screens off" time.
A brief check-in: "How was your day? What's on your mind?"
The same closing activities each night: brushing teeth, pajamas, plugging in devices, then reading for 10 minutes.

Over time, these small rituals add up to big signals.

4. Keep Bedrooms Dark, Quiet, and Device-Free

This step dives a little deeper into steps you can take to protect your child/teen's bedroom at night. In addition to removing or disabling electronics you might also consider the following:

Make sure bedrooms are cool. Our body temperature naturally drops 1-2 degrees during the night. A cool bedroom temperature around 65 degrees helps the body more easily reach that goal.

Make sure bedrooms are dark. Any kind of light at night can reduce melatonin and interfere with sleep. Avoiding light from TV screens, computer screens, and phone screens is very important. Blackout curtains also help eliminate the light from street lights.

Be mindful of exposure to sound. For those kids who like to go to sleep to the sound of a television or music try a fan or white noise machine instead. The variable volume between a show and its commercials, or within certain songs, can subtly but significantly disrupt quality sleep. The fluctuating volume keeps the brain on alert and prevents it from being able to fully relax into a deep sleep. A consistent noise like white noise machines or fans do not trigger vigilance in the brain and a deep, sound sleep is more easily achieved.

If your child has been sneaking devices at night, expect pushback. That doesn't mean you are doing the wrong thing; it means you are changing a pattern that has been rewarding to their tired brain.

If this feels impossible right now, start with partial steps:

Try moving the cut-off time earlier in the evening, even if devices are still in the bedroom for a while.
Removing the most problematic device first (usually the smartphone), then gradually adding others.

Even moderate changes in nighttime device use can lead to noticeable improvements in mood, mornings, and school functioning.

5. Watch Caffeine, Nicotine, and Sugar, Especially Later in the Day

Many modern kids are unknowingly wiring themselves for poor sleep by consuming:

Energy drinks
Highly caffeinated sodas
Sweetened coffees or teas
Vaping products that contain nicotine
High-sugar snacks in the evening

These substances:

Make it harder to fall asleep.
Disrupt quality sleep with mini-withdrawals and cravings.
Increase nighttime wakening that your child may not even fully remember.

You can help by:

Setting clear family rules around energy drinks and caffeine—especially after midday.
Talking with healthcare providers if nicotine, alcohol, or other substances are part of your teen's life.
Offering lower-sugar, higher-protein options in the evening—things like nuts, cheese, yogurt, eggs, or leftovers instead of candy or chips.

You do not have to police every bite or sip. But shifting the general pattern away from high stimulation in the late afternoon and evening can significantly improve sleep.

6. Model the Sleep Habits You Want to See

Your child is watching you, consciously or not.

If you are regularly:

Up past midnight scrolling or working
Falling asleep in front of a screen
Complaining about being exhausted but doing nothing to protect your own sleep

...it sends a double message: Sleep matters for you, but not for me.

Instead, where you can, let them see you taking your own sleep seriously:

"I'm heading to bed; I notice I'm much less patient when I don't sleep enough."
"I'm plugging my phone in out here; it's too easy for me to get sucked in if it's next to my bed."
"I've been in a better mood since I started going to bed 30 minutes earlier. You may notice I'm less cranky in the morning."

This is not about pretending to be perfect. It's about modeling a basic truth: Adults also have to work at healthy sleep, and it's worth the effort.

7. Watch for Signs of Sleep Deprivation

Finally, I encourage you to trust what you see. Signs that your child or teen may not be getting the sleep they need include:

Dark circles under their eyes. This is the sign I see most in schools.

Being chronically hard to wake up, no matter how early they went to bed on paper.
Falling asleep in class, in the car, or during any quiet moment.
Big mood swings, irritability, or meltdowns that seem out of proportion to the situation.
Constant cravings for junk food, sugar, or screens.
Frequent illnesses or taking a long time to recover from minor illnesses.

Before concluding, "They're just lazy," "They're just dramatic," or "They just need more discipline," pause and ask:

"Could this be a tired brain and body trying to cope?"

If the answer might be yes, prioritize sleep changes before layering on more consequences. When sleep improves, you will often see behavior and emotional regulation improve as well.

Putting It All Together

I know this is a lot. You are being asked to make changes in your own habits, your child's habits, and the overall structure of your household, all while living in a culture that is pushing in the opposite direction.

You are not expected to fix everything this week.

Here's a way to start:

Pick one step from the exit plan that feels most doable right now. Maybe it's creating a central charging station. Maybe it's shifting bedtime by 20 minutes. Maybe it's asking your child to give you a tour of their online world.

Explain why you are making that change, in simple, honest language.

Stick with it long enough to see what happens—not just for a few days, but for several weeks.

Adjust and add as you go. Once one change feels more normal, consider adding another.

You cannot change the entire digital environment your child is growing up in by yourself. That's why we also need better laws and protections at the national and global level.

But you can change what happens inside your own home.

You can create clearer expectations, safer nights, and healthier rhythms.

You can help your child reclaim their sleep—and with it, more of their mood, health, and ability to cope with a challenging world.

And you don't have to be a perfect parent to do it. You just have to be willing to take the next small, deliberate step.

Chapter 7
The Educator Exit Plan

School Structures to Support Mental Health and Avoid Digital Overuse

This chapter is written for my fellow educators. I consider educators to be anyone who works in schools. This includes district and school administrators, teachers, counselors, related service providers, paraprofessionals, nurses, clerks, custodians, cafeteria workers, etc. There is not one person in a school building that doesn't have the capacity to make a difference in the life of a young person. This chapter is written directly for you, but I encourage parents and legislators to also read this chapter to get a better understanding of how schools operate and the challenges they face.

While this chapter is written primarily to help change the educational environment for students in kindergarten through grade 12, many of the ideas in this chapter apply to undergraduate and graduate level students as well. Brains are brains. Nervous systems are nervous systems. And the effects of an overstimulating digital environment do not magically disappear at age eighteen.

I left K–12 education with a lot of mixed feelings. Watching students learn, grow, and mature into adults is one of the most rewarding experiences I can imagine. It is also an honor and a privilege to be entrusted with the care and development of other people's children. At the same time, I am painfully aware of the significant challenges educators face now.

Not only do you have the responsibility of getting students across the graduation stage, you also provide layers of care that were not historically assigned to schools. Many schools now feed students, provide clothing/transportation vouchers, and deliver emotional support on top of administrative, teaching, coaching, counseling, and case-management duties. You also carry the stress and fallout that happens when colleagues call out sick, go out on leave, or sustain injuries in environments that are increasingly high intensity. Smaller schools in particular can have their entire schedule thrown into disarray when just one person calls out sick.

That said, what I have seen at both the school and district level is nothing shy of impressive. If I worked with you directly, I know you are fully invested in student success, and I have seen you bust your tail in ways that at times seemed super human. You show up to face enormous challenges, despite the curve balls coming at you daily, because seeing students succeed is always worth the effort. I see this level of commitment across education and I am grateful to have chosen a profession that attracts people like you who persist in helping students thrive, regardless of the circumstances.

Despite the non-monetary rewards that come with educating youth, things in schools have become progressively more challenging each year. Students have much higher emotional needs and you often have inadequate time and resources to address these needs. The expectations placed on instructional time leaves little to no space to support other student needs—socialization, time outside, exercise, and relaxed access to quality nutrition and hydration. As students spend more time on devices and less time moving around, their health and mental health are increasingly compromised.

This chapter is a direct bridge from the Parent Exit Plan. In the previous chapter, I asked parents to create structure at home, protect sleep, and reduce the invisible overnight digital environment that many youth return to after "bedtime." In this chapter we will widen the lens and ask you as educators to think about the structures you provide to support student wellbeing.

If we start from the premise that schools can create environments that support healthy bodies and brains, we can reduce dysregulation and improve learning, without turning educators into therapists, and without inadvertently adding to digital overload.

Because here is the uncomfortable truth: even well-meaning school practices can unintentionally compound the problem. If students are already living in a high-dopamine, high-stimulation digital world, and then they come to school and spend most of the day on screens, devices, apps, and constant clicking/visual input, we may be reinforcing the exact patterns we are trying to interrupt.

That's why this chapter is about structures.

And because district administrators set the structures and expectations teachers have to work within, the first section is written for district leaders. The second section is written for educators in classrooms—the people who do the daily work of holding students steady and guiding them toward growth.

In previous chapters I spoke a lot about the importance of restoring students' sleep through health tech habits among other things. While I realize school officials cannot follow students home to ensure students store away their devices at night and get to bed on time, there are four tiers within the health hierarchy that schools can leverage to positively influence student wellbeing—tiers that help support quality sleep at home and promote emotional regulation and learning during the day. That's where we are going next.

District Level Exit Plan: System-Wide Structures to Support Mental Health and Learning

I want to start off by acknowledging a dynamic that may leave you as a district administrator questioning some of the things I recommend in this section. The dynamic is this -It is likely that you have never seen the level of disruption I talk about in this book. There may be a number of reasons for this. One reason could be that your district walk-throughs are designed to highlight the strengths of a school. In that case, district administrators will be shown the high-performing classrooms that are well managed and you will never see the challenges. Another reason could be the fact that principals are under a lot of pressure to have their students perform well, and many principals are not protected by a union. Since the relationship between principals and district administrators is disciplinary by design, this creates a built-in incentive for principals to put their best foot forward and avoid airing their school's dirty laundry to you.

When I used to go to schools to speak with principals I asked them not to airbrush things for me because doing so would compromise my ability to help them; but that was easier for me to do because I wasn't in a supervisory role with them. So, unless your district walkthroughs are designed to directly uncover problems of practice within the school, or your district has mental health screening data that informs you of the level of social emotional support your students need, some of the interventions I describe below may seem unnecessary. That said, I would strongly encourage you to read through both my recommendations and my rationale for them.

The next section is a suggested roadmap to building structures that support youth mental health.

1) Reduce Unnecessary Stimulation Across All Buildings

Establish structures and expectations that ensure a calm learning environment. District-level policies that can reduce stimulation and support healthy nervous systems can include:

-District-wide phone-free schools—including the adults. This is not about control. It's about nervous system protection.

Phones introduce:

- constant notifications
- social comparison
- group chat drama
- real-time documentation of mistakes
- immediate escape from discomfort

When phones are present, students' brains never fully settle into learning mode. They stay in a state of partial vigilance — always waiting for the next buzz.

Phone-free schools:

- reduce real-time peer conflict escalation
- limit filming, posting, and online humiliation

- help students relearn face-to-face interaction
- rebuild delayed gratification ("I can check later")

A phone-free district helps maintain consistency between school buildings, particularly in districts with high student mobility. It also prevents teachers from having to police phones in isolation and it protects teacher morale.

-Calming corners in every elementary classroom that include a variety of calming and self- regulation tools

-Structured options for downshifting in middle schools

-Lounge spaces in high schools where students can socialize in low-stimulation ways

-Eliminate all unnecessary stimuli. For example, walkie-talkies can be very disruptive to student well-being. Keep urgent communications away from student ears. Use ear devices so only those who are communicating can hear the messages.

2) Build Daily Movement into the Schedule and Make it a Requirement

Districts may want to consider providing structured opportunities such as:

- **40-60 minutes of daily exercise for elementary students**, ideally in two 20 to 30-minute blocks. Not 10. Not 15. Two real blocks where bodies can actually move.
- **At least 30 minutes of daily movement for middle and high school students**, outdoors when possible.

Movement supports the top tier on the health hierarchy by helping students optimize the way their bodies utilize oxygen. Exercise also provides students with the opportunity to physically develop, integrate learning, build muscle, improve blood flow, increase serotonin levels, and support quality sleep. But more importantly, when we're thinking about trying to support students' ability to tolerate being away from screens, movement is a great way to help them do that by providing their bodies with an outlet for the energy that has built up inside of them while sitting.

And to be very clear: I'm not talking about "more sports." I'm talking about movement as a foundational health intervention—one that benefits every student, including students who do not see themselves as athletes.

This can look like:

- consistent recess and movement blocks in elementary schools, protected from being removed for academics or behavior
- movement breaks embedded into class periods
- indoor alternatives during winter months
- active electives and rotating movement stations for older grades

If we continue to treat movement as optional, we will keep seeing students who cannot sit, cannot focus, and cannot regulate—and we will keep interpreting that as defiance rather than bodies begging for what they need to regulate and thrive.

3) Build in Time for Emotional Support and Identify Struggling Students Earlier

It is important to build time into the day when students can get emotional support. Many schools have blocks of time set aside when students can receive extra-help. Unfortunately, if a student also needs academic support, oftentimes the student's emotional needs get pushed to the sideline.

One way to ensure that all students with social emotional needs receive the appropriate support is to proactively identify them in the first place. Using a social emotional or mental health screening tool is the best way to accomplish this goal. Without a screening process in place, many students who need social emotional support are not easily identified. Sure, the cohort of students with significant behavioral challenges are easy to spot, but there are many others who suffer in silence and are easily missed when districts don't proactively screen. When we implemented mental health screening in my district, 70 percent of the students who screened in for being at risk for anxiety or depression had not been previously identified as needing support. Districts with many high performing students, may be at particular risk of under identifying and under serving the social emotional needs of their students, because their distress may be masked by high performance.

Social emotional or mental health screening can seem scary at first, but consider this thought: What we talk about and what we measure in schools sends just as loud a message as what we don't talk about. When we avoid screening students or avoid talking about mental health it not only perpetuates stigma and minimizes its importance, but it leaves a lot of students feeling invisible and/or misunderstood.

Districts routinely do vision screenings as well as a variety of other health-related screenings. With the national average for youth mental health challenges rising to 1 in 5 youth, it is time we make mental health screenings and follow up services standard practice.

4) Consider Later Start Times for High School

Teen development is intense during puberty, with rapid growth and brain changes. During this time, circadian rhythms in teens naturally shift to later [23]. A later start time for high school aligns better with biology and supports learning and mental health.

This is also relevant for teens involved in after-school activities that require late nights—games, performances, concerts. If we demand excellence from students while ignoring the sleep realities of their schedules, we are setting them up to struggle when we can be setting them up for success.

5) Ensure Access to Quality Water Throughout the Day

Supporting students on this tier of the health hierarchy is an infrastructure cost worth funding. In Massachusetts, roughly 70% of districts have schools with high lead levels, and around 30% have water with high copper content (based on widely reported statewide testing patterns) [24]. Disproportionately high levels of copper within the body are associated with an increased prevalence of depression and anxiety, so quality water is an important resource to consider for supporting youth mental health. Regular access to quality water helps circulate nutrients, supports brain function, and helps flush out toxins.

A nervous system is more likely to regulate—and a student is more likely to sleep well—when they are properly hydrated.

District actions that matter:

- invest in clean water stations that students can access easily
- make water access visible and normal (not something that requires teacher permission)
- ensure students are allowed to carry water bottles throughout the day

6) Budget for Cooks and Treat Food as Brain Fuel

Nutrition is an important tier on the health hierarchy since food serves as the building blocks for strong bodies and healthy minds. Districts may want to consider budgeting for cooks in addition to servers in cafeterias so students can benefit from freshly prepared quality meals rather than packaged, ultra-processed foods, which can contribute to nutritional deficiencies linked to mental health and behavioral challenges. [25] While this book does not attempt to solve nutritional inequities on its own, providing nutrient-dense foods is a great way to support youth, particularly those who do not have access to quality nutrition at home.

If your schools have vending machines, offer nutrient-dense foods and avoid junk. The details matter. Schools will have difficulty supporting mental health while offering constant access to ultra-processed, high stimulation foods that destabilize regulation. When we feed students meals that spike blood sugar, crash blood sugar, and provide little protein or micronutrients, we should not be surprised when we see:

- irritability
- emotional volatility
- "energy spikes" followed by shutdown
- attention instability

7) Stabilize Meal Schedules to Support Regulation

Ensure student meal times are consistent throughout the week.

When lunch is served at the same time every day for a given grade, it helps support a student's ability to self-regulate. Consistent meal schedules help stabilize functions across the day.

Rotating lunch time every few days to match academic rotations can be problematic for vulnerable students and can lead to emotional and energetic dysregulation. Regular meal times with quality food help regulate blood sugar, mood, and behavior.

This is a small structural change that can create meaningful downstream effects, especially for students who already live with instability.

8) Budget for After-School Activities to Replace Screens and Foster Connection

Budget for busing and after-school activities that involve movement and social interaction. This is one of the best ways school districts can provide alternatives to digital devices.

For districts with limited financial or staffing resources, consider using the last period of the day for socially connected activities. This could look like every teacher in the building running a class—or a club—around a high-interest extra-curricular activity.

That structure does a lot at once:

- teachers connect with students around mutually high-interest topics
- students build a mentor-type relationship with a staff member
- students socialize with peers with similar interests
- every student is meaningfully connected to at least one adult and one peer group

This is also a protective factor for attendance. Students are more likely to show up when they feel known and connected.

9) Design Indoor Environments for Movement and Natural Light

This step may not be necessary in areas that have a mild climate year-round, but in colder climates, where students cannot get outside regularly, districts may want to prioritize indoor spaces that allow movement—more gym space, larger classrooms, and open areas.

Also, so students do not miss out on the benefits of sunlight for circadian regulation, districts may want to consider building atrium-style spaces where students can eat or gather in natural light. The glass won't help increase their vitamin D levels, but it will provide the kind of light the body recognizes to support healthy sleep.

10) Consider System-wide Device Limits

For schools that issue devices, consider time limits at the system level. This means, once the time limit on a device is reached, the device automatically logs off. For devices that go home with students, districts can lock the devices during nighttime hours.

Setting limits like this helps teachers stay intentional about assigning device-based activities only when they truly make sense. With limits in place, transitioning away from devices becomes standard practice and helps alleviate the conflicts that arise when teachers are the ones asking students to get off their devices. Locking devices overnight also helps parents avoid battles with their kids and does not inadvertently reinforce bad habits at home.

Classroom Level Exit Plan: Designing Classrooms for Healthy Brains in a Digital Age

Before we get into specific strategies, I want to pause and acknowledge something that often goes unspoken.

By the time students walk through the school doors each morning, many of them have already spent years in a high-dopamine, high-stimulation digital environment. Their nervous systems have adapted to constant novelty, rapid feedback, and intense emotional input. For many students, especially those who have been online since early childhood, this environment has shaped not just their habits, but their brains.

So, when students arrive in classrooms that are quieter, slower, and require sustained attention, real life can feel unbearable by comparison.

If you've ever thought, *"Why can't they just sit?"* or *"Why does everything feel like a fight now?"* — you're not failing as an educator. You're seeing neuroadaptation in real time.

The goal here is not to compete with TikTok, gaming platforms, or social media for stimulation. That's a race you cannot win — and one you shouldn't run. **The goal is to rebuild tolerance for sustained attention, effort, frustration, and meaning** while protecting students from further digital overload during the school day.

That's what the strategies below are designed to do.

---

1. Make Your Classroom "Phone-Free"

You don't have to wait for district action to implement a "phone-free environment," in your classroom. If you have the classroom management skills to enforce it, I would encourage you to start now.

If you're doing this at the classroom level, consistency matters more than intensity.

You might say, calmly and repeatedly:

- "Phones go here at the start. That's just how class works."
- "I'm not mad. I'm holding the boundary."
- "We can talk about concerns after class, not during."

Expect resistance at first — not because students are defiant, but because removing phones produces mild withdrawal. That discomfort usually settles within a few weeks when boundaries are predictable and non-negotiable.

And one important reminder: **this works best when it is school-wide**. If you are the only teacher doing it, it might be a tough sell at first. My guess is students will eventually appreciate that you care enough to help them focus and learn. Besides, there are few things more demoralizing than trying to teach a lesson you prepped for hours while students are watching videos on their phones under their desks. So, this is a great way to protect your longevity as a teacher too.

---

2. Use Technology Intentionally

Technology is not the enemy. Reflexive use is.

One of the most common patterns I see in schools is technology being used not because it's the best tool, but because it keeps students quiet and compliant — at least temporarily.

The problem is that constant low-level stimulation:

- worsens attention over time
- increases irritability when devices are removed
- makes non-digital tasks feel intolerable

A helpful guiding question is:
"Is this technology serving learning — or serving classroom control?"

Intentional use looks like:

- slow tasks (writing, drafting, revising)
- research that requires synthesis, not clicking
- accessibility supports that genuinely remove barriers
- assessments that give meaningful feedback

And just as important: balance.

For every online task, try to include:

- discussion
- handwriting

- reading from paper
- movement
- peer interaction

You might say to students:

- "We're doing this part on paper so your brain gets a break."
- "This assignment doesn't need a screen — and that's on purpose."
- "You're not being punished; we're training focus."

When students push back — and some will — that's often a sign you're doing something right.

---

3. Replace Passive Instruction with Active, High-Meaning Engagement

This is one of the most important sections of this chapter.

For students who have adapted to fast, high-stimulation input, long passive lectures and repetitive worksheets often feel physically painful. Not boring — painful.

The solution is not to make everything entertaining. It's to make learning **active, meaningful, and neurologically rewarding**.

Neurologist-turned-educator Dr. Judy Willis has written extensively about how learning actually changes the brain [26]. Her work emphasizes that dopamine — the neurotransmitter associated with motivation — is released not through speed or flash, but through:

- curiosity
- prediction
- effort
- progress
- mastery

In other words, the brain lights up when students *work toward* understanding — not when information is simply delivered.

Active engagement might look like:

- starting lessons with a question instead of an explanation
- asking students to predict outcomes before revealing answers
- revisiting predictions later ("Who wants to revise their thinking?")
- letting students wrestle with problems briefly before instruction

You might say:

- "Before I explain this, what do you think will happen?"
- "Turn to someone and argue the opposite position."
- "Write down your guess — we'll come back to it."

These moments create healthy dopamine — the kind tied to learning, not addiction.

You may notice initial frustration. That's okay. Frustration is often the doorway to deeper learning — as long as students feel safe and supported.

---

4. Connect Learning to Students' Interests and Identities

Brains pay attention to what feels relevant.

When learning feels disconnected from students' lives, motivation drops — and the brain looks for stimulation elsewhere.

Connecting learning to identity does **not** mean lowering standards. It means offering meaningful entry points.

Examples:

- allowing students to choose topics within a shared objective
- letting students explore content through cultural, community, or personal lenses
- offering multiple formats for demonstrating understanding

You might say:

- "The skill is the same. The topic is your choice."

- "How does this show up in your world?"
- "Where have you seen this before?"

This kind of relevance increases engagement and reduces the need for external stimulation.

It also sends a powerful message: *you matter here.*

---

5. Borrow the Healthy Parts of Gaming (Without Screens)

This section is directly informed by Judy Willis's work and is foundational.

Many students who struggle in traditional classrooms thrive in games — not because of screens, but because of structure.

Games provide:

- clear goals
- immediate feedback
- achievable challenge
- visible progress
- a sense of competence

Dr. Willis explains that these elements trigger dopamine through effort and success, not novelty. That's the kind of dopamine that strengthens learning circuits instead of eroding them.

You can replicate this without technology.

In classrooms, this looks like:

- clear daily goals ("By the end of class, you'll be able to…")
- breaking large tasks into visible steps
- frequent feedback ("You're on the right track.")
- increasing challenge once mastery is shown

You might say:

- "You've mastered level one — here's the next challenge."

- "That mistake tells me your brain is stretching."
- "Let's track progress, not perfection."

This approach shifts students from *avoiding work* to *working toward success.*

It also reduces learned helplessness, which is increasingly common in digitally overwhelmed students.

---

6. Build Collaboration and Peer Connection into the Day

Digital life has changed how students relate to each other. Many students feel simultaneously over-connected online and deeply disconnected in person.

Classrooms can become places where students relearn how to be in community.

Intentional collaboration matters.

This means:

- clear roles in group work
- explicit teaching of collaboration skills
- rotating partners to prevent isolation
- debriefing how collaboration went

Social connection is a powerful regulator of stress. When students feel they belong, attendance improves, behavior stabilizes, and learning deepens.

---

7. Make Movement Non-Negotiable

Movement is not a break from learning. It is part of learning.

Movement:

- increases oxygen to the brain
- supports dopamine regulation
- improves mood and attention

- reduces agitation

Simple strategies:

- stand-and-stretch moments
- gallery walks
- moving to stations
- learning outdoors when possible

If you're worried about losing control, remember this: **movement often prevents bigger disruptions later**.

---

8. Use Low-Tech Tools to Engage Every Student

One of the most effective tools I've seen is also one of the simplest: individual whiteboards.

Ask a question.
Everyone answers.
Everyone participates.

This:

- increases engagement
- gives immediate feedback
- prevents passive disengagement
- helps students tolerate slower pacing

It also reduces anxiety for students who fear being called out.

---

9. Stop Using Screens as "Breaks"

When students are dysregulated, screens often worsen the cycle.

Instead, offer:

- hands on or movement activities whenever possible
- breathing exercises

- drawing
- stretching
- quiet reading
- sensory tools

Teach regulation explicitly. Practice it before it's needed.

You might say:

- "We're giving your nervous system a reset."
- "This will feel boring at first — that's okay."

---

10. Teach Conflict Resolution and Digital Citizenship

Many school crises are rooted in conflict—often conflict that begins or explodes online.

You might also consider adding a conflict resolution corner in your classroom, with rules and expectations for how disagreements will be resolved. Doing something like this normalizes the fact that conflict happens, even between the best of friends, and the expectation is that you face the conflict head on. To do this schools can:

- implement structured conflict resolution processes
- teach digital citizenship explicitly
- normalize conflict as manageable, not shameful

Teach:

- how to handle group chats
- how to respond to online cruelty without escalating
- how to understand the permanence of posting
- how to ask for help before problems become crises

When students have the knowledge and skills they need, behavior improves. When they don't, adults spend the day putting out fires.

A "Random Tuesday" and Why This Can't Rest on Teachers' Shoulders

Before I close this chapter, I want to step out of "strategy mode" for a minute and speak to you more directly.

If you're reading this and thinking, *"This all sounds good, but my reality is chaos,"* I want you to know something: that reaction does not mean you're resistant to change. It means you're a realist.

There are days in schools now that feel like triage from the first bell to the last.

So, let me paint a picture—not because you need more proof that things are hard, but because when we name the reality, the solutions stop sounding like "nice ideas" and start sounding like what they actually are: protective structures for human nervous systems.

Imagine a fairly ordinary Tuesday.

First period starts and three students arrive late. One is angry because a group chat exploded overnight. Another is silent and flat, barely able to make eye contact. A third is jittery and impulsive—talking loudly, laughing too hard, bouncing in their seat—because they slept four hours and then chugged an energy drink on the way in.

Two minutes into your opener, a phone buzzes. Then another. A student glances down, tries to hide it, and now you can feel the energy shift. Half the class is scanning, wondering what's happening. You haven't even taught yet, and already their brains are in social-monitoring mode.

You do what you always do. You redirect. You move closer. You use your teacher voice. You try to stay warm, calm, and steady—because you know that's what regulation looks like. You're not trying to "win." You're trying to keep the room stable.

Then it happens: a student refuses a direction. Not with a big dramatic outburst—almost worse than that—with a flat, dismissive "no." Now you have to decide: do you correct it (and risk escalation), or do you keep teaching (and risk sending the message that boundaries don't exist)?

This is the invisible burden teachers carry all day: a thousand micro-decisions that are really decisions about nervous systems.

Somewhere in the middle of all this, you still have learning targets. You still have standards. You still have pacing. You still have the pressure of "coverage." And you're doing it in a room full of brains that have been trained by the digital environment to expect immediate reward, immediate feedback, immediate escape from discomfort.

So, when I say "reduce screen time," or "build active engagement," or "borrow the healthy parts of gaming," I am not naïve about what I'm asking you to do.

I'm asking you to do something brave: hold the line for real life.

Real life is slower than a feed. Real life requires frustration tolerance. Real life asks students to stay with something even when it isn't instantly gratifying. Real life asks them to read facial expressions, repair conflict, and keep going when they don't feel like it.

And right now, many students are coming to school with less capacity for real life—not because they're weak, or lazy, or broken, but because they are developing inside an environment that has been engineered to hijack attention.

If you've felt yourself becoming less patient than you used to be, or more exhausted, or more brittle by the end of the day, I want you to hear this clearly:

That is not a character flaw. That is what happens when you spend years trying to regulate a dysregulated environment.

Teachers are not just teaching content anymore. You are constantly doing nervous-system leadership, whether anyone names it or not. You are absorbing emotional spillover that used to be buffered by time outdoors, in-person friendships, family dinners, boredom, free play, and sleep.

So, if this chapter feels heavy, it's because the job is heavy.

Now, here's the hopeful part.

Even on a day like that Tuesday, small structural changes can shift the whole room.

You decide that phones go into a pouch at the start of class, every day, with the same calm script:

> "Phones go here. You're not in trouble. This is how we protect learning in this room."

You expect pushback for a while. You don't take it personally. You treat it like building a muscle: uncomfortable at first, stronger over time.

You stop using screens as "breaks" and instead create two regulation options students can choose from when they're escalating:

> "You can take two minutes to reset. Option A: breathe at the back table. Option B: a quick walk to the water fountain and back. Your job is to come back ready."

You start class more often with a prediction question rather than an explanation, because you're trying to trigger curiosity and the kind of dopamine that comes from meaning and mastery—not stimulation:

> "Before I teach this, I want your best guess. What do you think happens if…?"

And you build in a short collaborative moment—not to be trendy, but because peer connection is a regulator:

> "Turn to the person next to you. Your job is to come up with one example from real life. I'll call on pairs, not individuals."

None of this turns a hard day into an easy day.

But it changes the tone.

It creates a classroom that says: *We do real life here. We practice being human here. You don't have to be entertained to be okay.*

And here is why I'm adding this section—because this is the part I never want you to miss:

Even if you do all of this beautifully, it cannot rest on you alone.

If the larger environment continues to intensify—if devices become more persuasive, more immersive, more sexually explicit, more socially punishing—schools will keep absorbing the downstream effects.

Teachers can build incredible protective factors. Schools can create healthier structures. Parents can create safer homes.

But the truth is: we are asking individual adults to hold back a tidal wave that is being generated upstream by design.

That is why the legislative chapter matters.

Not because teachers aren't doing enough. Not because parents aren't doing enough. Not because clinicians aren't doing enough.

The legislative chapter matters because legislators are the ones who can make the upstream changes needed to make your work sustainable; changes that redesign the environment so schools are not forced to function as the final containment zone for an unregulated digital world.

Why This Can't Be the School's Job Alone

If you've stayed with me this far, you might be thinking something like: *"Okay. I can do some of this in my classroom and our school can do some of this, but we can't do all of this."*

Exactly.

Schools were never designed to be the primary buffer between children and a powerful commercial environment. Schools were designed to educate.

They were designed to socialize. They were designed to help young people become capable citizens and adults.

What has happened over the past decade is that schools have slowly become the place where society sends problems it doesn't know how to solve—hunger, housing instability, family stress, untreated mental health challenges, and now, a digital environment that is shaping development in ways we are still trying to understand.

So, when we talk about reducing screen overload, rebuilding attention, improving regulation, and restoring real-world connection, it's important to name the limits.

Even the best school culture cannot override an environment that follows kids home, climbs into bed with them, and stays with them through the night.

That's why this book is structured the way it is.

Parents can do meaningful work at home—especially around sleep, device boundaries, and replacing screens with real-world rhythms.

Educators can do meaningful work during the school day—especially around structure, engagement, movement, connection, and reducing unnecessary digital exposure in classrooms.

But neither parents nor educators should be asked to fight a multi-billion-dollar attention economy alone.

Teachers should not have to compete with algorithms that are optimized to keep kids hooked.

Administrators should not have to spend their days policing devices that were intentionally designed to undermine focus and self-control.

And students should not have to use willpower they do not yet biologically possess to resist a system built to bypass willpower.

This is the point where a society has to decide what it is willing to protect.

We already accept, without debate, that there are things children should not have unlimited access to—because their brains are still developing. We put boundaries around tobacco, alcohol, gambling, certain medications, cars, and workplace hazards. We do not call that "anti-freedom." We call it child protection.

The digital environment is now one of the most influential developmental environments children live in.

If we want the strategies in this chapter to work at scale—and not just in isolated classrooms led by heroic educators—then the upstream environment has to change.

That is why the next chapter matters; not as a political argument, but as a public health argument, a child development argument, and an infrastructure argument.

Parents can change what happens inside a home. Educators can change what happens inside a school day.

And legislators can change what happens in the environment *around* both.

That's where we're going next.

Chapter 8
A Legal Framework to Protect Children in the Digital Age

The Missing Piece in Our National Strategy

Whenever a society faces a widespread public-health threat, there comes a point when individual solutions simply cannot solve a systemic problem. Parents cannot parent their way out of a toxic environment. Teachers cannot teach their way out of a structurally unsafe system. Clinicians cannot treat their way out of a societal exposure that is engineered to overwhelm the frontal lobe of developing children.

We have reached that point with youth and the digital environment.

I spent over three decades working with youth—walking hallways, sitting with families in their living rooms, working with medically fragile teenagers, supporting school counselors who were stretched to their limits, and watching year after year as the digital world grew louder, faster, more intrusive, and more developmentally mismatched for children. There were days I felt like I was standing at the opening of a well with a hundred children calling out for help at the bottom of the well, with no rope to throw them.

Parents are trying. Educators are trying. Health professionals are trying. But none of us can compete with an industry whose profits depend on capturing the attention of the young brain before that brain has developed the capacity to use discernment or restraint.

Over roughly the last decade, our national response has been to spend more on mental health. Federal and state behavioral-health budgets have climbed dramatically [27]. Schools have added counselors and social workers, hospitals have expanded psychiatric units, and emergency departments have created mental-health pods for children and adolescents. Yet the curves that matter most have not bent in the direction we hoped. Rates of adolescent depression and persistent sadness have climbed, not fallen. Mental-health–related emergency visits for youth have increased, not decreased. Suicide attempts and self-harm have become more common, not less. In other words, we have built a larger and larger downstream response to an upstream problem that is still accelerating.

This chapter starts from a hard but necessary truth: **the current digital environment is destroying our kids and we cannot treat our way out of an environment that continues to manufacture distress faster than we can respond to it.** If the only tool we reach for is "more services," the best we can expect will be to keep spending more money while watching more children fall through the cracks or worse yet, pay the ultimate price.

This chapter is written for those who hold legislative authority—the people who can help redesign the environment our children live in. It is not a blame-based chapter. It is not anti-technology. It is pro-child, pro-development, and pro-future. It comes from a place of deep respect for everyone involved: parents who feel lost, teachers who feel overwhelmed, children who are suffering, and even tech executives who never imagined the collateral damage their tools would create. It also comes from my 33 years of clinical experience working with youth. Keep in mind, I am a glass half-full kind of person. I don't spook easily, and I often persist in tackling problems long after everyone else has given up. So, when I raise a white flag it means the situation is really serious. **We have to make changes or many of our kids won't make it**, I am not being dramatic. I am giving you the hard truth.

I am not saying technology has to be eliminated. I'm saying it needs boundaries, structured access, and developmental alignment.

And, most importantly, it needs rules.

Rules are what finally turned the tide with tobacco.
Rules are what saved lives with car seats and seat belts.
Rules are what reshaped food labeling, lead exposure, and prescription safety.

And rules—carefully crafted, ethically grounded, and developmentally informed—can reshape our digital environment too.

That is where legislators come into play, because they hold the master key that can make these changes a reality.

The good news is: legislators do not have to start from scratch. A global movement has begun. The United Kingdom, the European Union, and many U.S. states have taken first steps toward online-safety regulations. And in 2024, Australia enacted one of the boldest child online-safety measures to date, requiring covered social media platforms to take reasonable steps to prevent children under 16 from holding accounts. The law recognizes that children's access to high-risk digital environments should not be governed solely by industry practices or individual parental supervision. That single decision, abroad, is already shifting the global discussion. It tells us something powerful: the world is moving. Momentum is building. And the United States cannot afford to fall behind.

What follows is a clear, step-by-step legislative roadmap for how lawmakers can steer us out of the youth mental health crisis by redesigning the digital environment at its structural roots. This chapter offers both policy rationale and practical strategy. A separate chapter will provide full model-legislative language that can be used in federal or state bills.

This is how we create an exit plan—not just for individual families, but for society.

Why Legislative Action Is Necessary

1. The Digital Environment Has Outpaced Developmental Science

Brain development follows a predictable pattern. Executive function, impulse control, working memory, and risk-assessment capacities develop gradually and are nowhere near complete in middle school. Even high school students are still navigating emotional, social, and neurochemical volatility.

Technology, meanwhile, is designed for fully formed adult brains—and even those adult brains struggle to manage it as well.

A child's nervous system, especially under the influence of reward-loop algorithms, is simply no match for the infinite scroll, the dopamine-engineered "recommended for you" feed, and the social comparison machinery of modern platforms. It is akin to asking a nine-year-old to walk into a casino, manage a credit card, or drive a car on the highway.

We would never expect a child to regulate their way through adult-engineered hazards without guardrails. Yet that is precisely what we have done with digital technology.

2. The Tobacco Paradigm: A Useful Analogy—But Not a Perfect One

When tobacco control advocates first raised alarms about youth smoking, the problem was clear: a product harmful by design was being aggressively marketed to an underdeveloped population. Policymakers required decades of data, hearings, courage, and public pressure to implement what should have been obvious protections.

But once the legal architecture was in place—age restrictions, advertising bans, label warnings, and liability standards—youth smoking rates plummeted.

Technology is more complex. It is beneficial when used appropriately and harmful when misaligned with development. But the structural lessons are the same:

- Youth need age-gated access.
- Companies must be responsible for the design of their products.
- Advertising to minors must be restricted.
- Education must accompany regulation.
- A "duty of care" must be codified.

The U.S. did not eliminate tobacco. It regulated it for children. We must now do the same with digital technology.

3. The Patchwork Problem

Today's digital-safety landscape is a patchwork of:

- Federal statutes that predate algorithmic feeds (COPPA, 1998)
- State laws that vary widely in scope
- Voluntary industry measures that lack enforcement
- Parental-control tools that shift responsibility away from the manufacturer and onto the overwhelmed family

The patchwork approach is failing. It is leaving children at risk, parents frustrated, and schools absorbing the emotional fallout.

A coherent national framework is overdue.

4. Changing the Digital Environment Is the Key That Unlocks Everything Else

Clinicians across the country are reporting the same patterns:

- Rising anxiety
- Social withdrawal
- Increased irritability
- Sleep disruption
- Exposure to adult content
- Online victimization
- Reduction in healthy movement, play, and offline exploration

We can invest billions in mental health services—and we should—but if the environment continues to work against children's neurobiology, we are merely building bigger rescue teams instead of stopping children from falling into the well in the first place.

Legislators have the unique authority to change the environment itself. Parents cannot do this. Teachers cannot do this. Even tech companies will not do this unless required to do so.

This is where policymakers become the decisive force for public health.

Principles for Developmentally Aligned Digital Policy

After working with families for decades, and studying the intersection of neurobiology, psychology, and technology, I've come to believe that digital policy should follow five developmental principles:

1. **Younger children require complete protection from independent internet access.**
2. **Pre-teens require structured education before independence.**
3. **Teens require phased freedom tied to maturity, responsibility, and life transitions.**
4. **Algorithms should never manipulate the developing brain.**
5. **Companies that profit from children's attention must have a legal duty of care.**

These principles are not ideological. They are practical. They support the real-world needs of children, families, schools, and communities.

They also form the backbone of the legislative roadmap that follows.

Chapter 9
The Legislative Exit Plan

This chapter translates developmental science into actionable legislative steps. It is intentionally actionable: legislators can pick up this roadmap and immediately understand where to begin.

Step 1: Prohibit Internet-Connected Devices and Toys for Elementary-Aged Children

Elementary-aged children should not have independent access to the internet. No algorithm. No public platform. No unfiltered content. No open digital world. It is simply too dangerous.

To accomplish this, legislators should:

- Prohibit the sale or marketing of internet-connected toys/products designed for ages 5–11.
- Require strict "safe mode" restrictions for any device used in schools.
- Require clear labeling so parents understand exactly what a device can and cannot do.

This step alone dramatically reduces exposure to inappropriate content, predator access, and algorithmic manipulation during a vulnerable neurological period.

Step 2: Require Digital-Safety Certification Before Middle-School Students Gain Independent Access

Just as teens must pass a written exam before driving, students should pass a **digital-literacy and online-safety competency test** before being granted independent internet access.

Legislation should require:

- A nationally standardized curriculum
- Instruction on privacy, social etiquette, data protection, identifying predators, and how algorithms work
- An assessment required between grades 6–8
- No independent school-based internet access until the test is passed

Middle school is where impulsivity peaks and executive function lags. Education—prior to independence—is crucial.

Step 3: Delay Smartphones Until Age 16

Smartphones are not phones. They are portable hyper-connected supercomputers with social comparison engines, commercial surveillance tools, and dopamine-driven feeds. They demand emotional regulation capacity that young teens simply do not have.

Legislation should:

- Prohibit smartphones for minors under age 16
- Allow exceptions only for work, driving, or documented medical necessity
- Require default safe-mode settings on devices for all minors under 18
- Build on emerging international precedent, including Australia's under-16 social media account restrictions, while addressing the broader risks created by unrestricted smartphone access.

This age threshold aligns with a major developmental transition: driving, employment, and a maturing identity.

Step 4: Reform Algorithmic Design for Minors

Algorithms should not be allowed to feed more of what a youth lingers on or scrolls through. This is how youth get exposed to increasingly extreme content and fall into problematic loops.

Legislation should require that:

- Children under 16 receive **search-only** results—no algorithmic recommendations
- High-schoolers have algorithmic feeds switched off by default
- Opt-in (not opt-out) consent is required
- Platforms undergo annual third-party audits of their child-impact risks

This step alone reshapes the digital terrain from a predator-rich, variable-reward environment into something far closer to a static library index.

Step 5: Prohibit Targeted Advertising to Minors

Minors should not be micro-targeted based on:

- Their browsing history
- Their vulnerabilities
- Their social interests
- Their emotional states

This mirrors the tobacco advertising ban. It also mirrors restrictions on alcohol, cannabis, gambling, and pharmaceuticals.

Minors are not fair game for behavioral advertising. And parents cannot defeat this system on their own.

Step 6: Assign Liability and Enforcement Authority

A law without enforcement is an aspiration, not a protection.

Legislation must:

- Assign oversight to the Federal Trade Commission
- Authorize state attorneys general to enforce violations
- Create civil penalties substantial enough to deter noncompliance (the tobacco model)
- Allow parents to bring lawsuits when harm occurs

This is where accountability begins to shift from the family to the system—where it belongs.

Step 7: Launch a National Education, Awareness, and Implementation Campaign

Policy alone won't change behavior. Education must accompany legislation.

This includes:

- Public education campaigns for parents
- School-based professional development
- Guidance for pediatricians, clinicians, and community groups
- Resources for tech companies to retool their products and algorithms

This is part of an ethical rollout: helping the public adapt rather than surprising them with mandates.

How This Mirrors Successful Public-Health Strategies

When it comes to protecting children, the U.S. has done this before:

- Lead paint bans
- Car seat and seatbelt laws
- Safe-sleep campaigns
- School vaccination requirements
- Tobacco and alcohol restrictions
- Food labeling requirements

In each case, five things were true:

1. The harm was widespread.
2. Parents could not prevent it on their own.
3. Industry profited from the exposure.
4. The public demanded action.
5. Legislation shifted norms and expectations.

Digital-safety policy follows the same pattern. It is a classic public-health problem disguised as a technological one.

Anticipating Opposition with Compassion and Clarity

Tech Industry Concerns

Many technology developers genuinely believe they build tools to help the world. They do not see themselves as harming children, and I believe most of them would welcome the guardrails if the entire industry had to comply equally.

Legislators should expect concerns about:

- Innovation constraints
- Profitability impact
- Feasibility of algorithmic reforms
- Constitutional questions about free speech

Compassion and clarity are both essential. The goal is not to punish tech companies—it is to align their innovations with child and adolescent development.

Parent Concerns

Parents are exhausted. Many feel guilty. The last thing they need is another narrative telling them they should have done more. Legislative reform lifts the burden off parents. It levels the playing field.

Youth Concerns

Adolescents may initially push back, but they will adapt; similar to the adaptation needed in 1984 when the drinking age changed from 18 to 21. We know from sleep research, mental health studies, and digital-health interventions: kids eventually feel better when their environment becomes healthier.

A Glimpse at International Momentum

Australia's decision to establish under-16 social media account restrictions is significant.

It signals that:

- The world is awakening to the developmental mismatch
- Developmentally based digital protections are becoming a legitimate public-policy response.
- A major democracy is willing to act decisively
- The U.S. risks falling behind in protecting children and youth

International movement often precedes U.S. change. Legislators should feel neither isolated nor timid. The global tide is rising.

Legislators Hold the Levers That Can Change Everything

Parents can set boundaries. Educators can teach skills. Clinicians can support healing. But none of these groups can redesign the ecosystem that is shaping the mental and emotional future of an entire generation.

Only legislators can do that.

We changed the future once when we decided children should not be exposed to tobacco. We changed it again when we required car seats, banned lead, and mandated safe sleep education. Each time, the nation became healthier.

We stand at that same threshold now—but the product is digital, not chemical.

The world is watching. Australia is already moving. The U.K. has acted. The E.U. is acting. U.S. states are stepping forward.

This is not the moment to be cautious. It is the moment to be courageous. Our children are not asking for perfection. They are asking for protection. And with the right legislative framework, we can finally give it to them.

Chapter 10
Model Legislation

The Children's Internet Product and Platform Safety Act (CIPPSA)

A Legislative Blueprint for Protecting Children Online

The policy chapter you have just read outlines *why* the United States needs a developmentally aligned digital-safety framework. This chapter provides the *how.* It is designed for lawmakers, advocacy organizations, education leaders, and parent coalitions seeking clear statutory language they can adapt and introduce in their own jurisdictions.

The following model legislation—The Children's Internet Product and Platform Safety Act (CIPPSA)—reflects the core principles described earlier:

1. **Elementary-aged children require a fully protected online environment.**
2. **Middle-school students must demonstrate digital-safety competence before they are allowed independent access.**
3. **High-school students benefit from phased, age-appropriate digital autonomy.**
4. **Algorithms and targeted advertising must not exploit the developing brain.**
5. **Technology companies must share responsibility for child safety.**

This sample bill is intentionally written at the federal level because if we are going to stop the youth mental health crisis, these proposed changes need to be nationwide.

A Model Bill for Congressional Consideration

SECTION 1. THE CHILDREN'S INTERNET PRODUCT AND PLATFORM SAFETY ACT (CIPPSA)

SECTION 2. FINDINGS AND PURPOSES

(a) Findings.

Congress (or the Legislature) finds that:

1. Children's neurodevelopment makes them uniquely vulnerable to online risks, including exposure to harmful content, predatory behavior, addictive platform design, and psychological manipulation through algorithmic recommendation systems.
2. A growing body of research demonstrates that early independent access to the internet contributes to increased rates of anxiety, sleep disruption, depression, cyber-victimization, and compulsive use patterns among minors.
3. Parents, guardians, schools, and clinicians cannot alone mitigate these risks when technology products are engineered with design features that exploit attention, vulnerability, and immature impulse-control.
4. Internet-connected products designed for elementary-aged children introduce developmental risks that cannot be sufficiently mitigated through parental controls or voluntary industry measures.
5. Middle-school students require comprehensive digital-safety education before being expected to navigate unsupervised online environments.
6. High-school students benefit from phased, developmentally-appropriate autonomy. International measures such as Australia's under 16 social media account restrictions demonstrate growing recognition that children and younger adolescents require stronger protections in digital environments. Smartphone restrictions provide additional protection by addressing risks that extend beyond social media platforms.

7. Targeted advertising to minors exploits their developmental vulnerabilities and contributes to unhealthy consumer behavior and psychological stress.
8. A comprehensive regulatory framework is necessary to ensure child-appropriate digital environments, clarify industry responsibilities, and protect the health, privacy, and wellbeing of minors across the United States.

(b) Purposes.

The purposes of this Act are to:

1. Establish minimum national safety standards for all digital products accessible to minors.
2. Prevent the manufacture or sale of internet-connected toys or devices intended for elementary-aged children.
3. Require digital-safety literacy and competency testing for middle-school students as a condition of independent internet access.
4. Restrict smartphone possession among minors under age 16 unless documented parental justification is provided.
5. Regulate algorithmic content delivery for minors and prohibit exploitative recommendation systems.
6. Prohibit targeted advertising to minors.
7. Impose transparency, auditing, and enforcement obligations on technology companies.
8. Promote a public-health approach that protects children without unduly burdening parents or schools.

SECTION 3. DEFINITIONS

For the purposes of this Act:

1. **"Minor"** means any person under 18 years of age.
2. **"Elementary-aged child"** means a minor age 11 or younger.
3. **"Middle-school-aged student"** means a minor approximately age 12 to 14.

4. **"High-school-aged student"** means a minor approximately age 15 to 17.
5. **"Internet-connected product or toy"** means any device, toy, tool, or object designed for, marketed to, or reasonably expected to be used by children that connects to the internet or transmits data beyond a closed educational network.
6. **"Independent internet access"** means access to the open internet without continuous direct supervision of a parent, guardian, educator, or designated adult.
7. **"Recommendation algorithm"** means any automated system, including AI-driven systems, that curates, prioritizes, or presents content based on user behavior, engagement, inferred preferences, or predicted interest.
8. **"Targeted advertising"** means advertising based on personal data, profiling, behavior, browsing history, engagement patterns, demographic inference, or psychographic prediction of a minor.
9. **"Safe-mode device"** means a digital device configured with restricted functionality, limited network access, and no algorithmic feed.

SECTION 4. PROHIBITION ON INTERNET-CONNECTED PRODUCTS FOR ELEMENTARY-AGED CHILDREN

(a) General Prohibition.

No manufacturer, technology company, distributor, or retailer shall design, develop, market, sell, or otherwise offer any internet-connected product or toy intended for use by elementary-aged children.

(b) Limited Exceptions.

A product may be exempt from this prohibition only if:

1. It connects exclusively to a closed, school-supervised network;
2. It prohibits open internet browsing;
3. It lacks any algorithmic recommendation system; and

4. It receives explicit certification from the designated federal agency as compliant with child-safety standards.

(c) Labeling Requirement.

Any permitted product under subsection (b) must display clear labeling stating:

- "This device does not provide access to the open internet," and
- "This device complies with the Children's Internet Product and Platform Safety Act."

SECTION 5. DIGITAL-SAFETY EDUCATION AND COMPETENCY TESTING FOR MIDDLE-SCHOOL STUDENTS

(a) Instruction.

Schools receiving federal funding shall provide annual, standardized digital literacy and safety instruction addressing:

1. Online predatory behavior and grooming recognition;
2. Privacy protection and personal data management;
3. Safe digital communication and civility;
4. Risks associated with misinformation and harmful content;
5. Understanding algorithmic design and behavioral manipulation;
6. Healthy technology habits, sleep awareness, and screen-time management.

(b) Competency Assessment.

1. All middle-school students shall complete a **Digital Safety Competency Test** between grades 6 and 8.
2. A student must pass the assessment before receiving independent internet access via school-issued devices or networks.
3. States may supplement or exceed federal standards, provided such standards remain consistent with the minimum curricular requirements.

SECTION 6. HIGH-SCHOOL INTERNET AND SMARTPHONE ACCESS REGULATIONS

(a) Age Restriction.

No minor under age 16 shall possess or be provided a smartphone capable of unrestricted internet access.

(b) Exceptions.

A smartphone may be issued to a minor under age 16 only if:

1. The minor has obtained a driver's license;
2. The minor has secured part-time employment requiring digital communication; or
3. A parent or guardian demonstrates a compelling need for early access, documented in writing such as for medical reasons i.e. continuous glucose monitoring.

(c) Device Requirements for Minors Under Age 18.

Any smartphone sold or activated for use by a minor shall include:

1. Default safe-mode restrictions;
2. Disabled targeted advertising functions;
3. Disabled recommendation algorithms unless explicitly opt-in by a parent or guardian;
4. Parental-access controls accessible without additional cost.

SECTION 7. ALGORITHMIC SAFEGUARDS AND SEARCH-ONLY REQUIREMENTS FOR MINORS

(a) Recommendation System Restrictions.

1. No platform or device shall employ a recommendation algorithm for users known or reasonably suspected to be under age 16.
2. Content shown to such users shall be limited to:
    - Direct search results; and
    - Chronological, non-personalized feeds.

(b) High-School Algorithmic Access.

For minors age 16 or older:

1. Recommendation algorithms shall be disabled by default;
2. Activation may occur only upon explicit opt-in by the user or guardian;
3. Platforms must provide clear, accessible disclosures about the risks associated with algorithmic content.

(c) Algorithmic Transparency and Auditing.

1. Technology companies shall submit annual third-party audit reports evaluating the child-safety impact of their algorithms.
2. Summaries of such audits shall be made publicly available.
3. Companies shall provide a mechanism for researchers and regulators to review algorithmic systems relevant to minors.

SECTION 8. PROHIBITION OF TARGETED ADVERTISING TO MINORS

(a) General Ban.

No company may deliver targeted advertising to minors.

(b) Age Uncertainty Standard.

Where a platform cannot reliably determine a user's age, it shall default to the protections afforded to minors.

(c) Enforcement.

Violations shall constitute unfair or deceptive acts under the Federal Trade Commission Act, subject to civil penalties.

SECTION 9. ENFORCEMENT, LIABILITY, AND PENALTIES

(a) Federal Enforcement Authority.

The Federal Trade Commission shall enforce this Act.

(b) State Enforcement Authority.

State Attorneys General may bring civil actions on behalf of residents to enforce compliance and recover penalties.

(c) Civil Penalties.

Violations of this Act may result in:

1. Fines up to $50,000 per affected minor per violation;
2. Mandatory corrective action plans;
3. Public disclosure of violations;
4. Suspension of product sales or platform operations for repeated or egregious violations.

(d) Private Right of Action.

Parents and guardians may bring civil suits for damages arising from violations of this Act, including emotional, psychological, or developmental harm to their child.

SECTION 10. IMPLEMENTATION TIMELINE

1. Regulatory rulemaking shall commence within 12 months of enactment.
2. Technology companies and manufacturers shall comply with all provisions within 24 months of final rulemaking.
3. Digital-safety curricula and competency testing shall be implemented by schools within 36 months of enactment.
4. Periodic review of this Act shall occur every 3 years.

SECTION 11. PERIODIC REVIEW AND ADAPTATION

A designated interagency council—including the Federal Trade Commission, the Department of Education, the Department of Health and Human Services, and independent child-development experts—shall:

1. Review compliance data and emerging technologies;
2. Recommend updates to age categories and safety provisions;
3. Submit reports to Congress every 3 years to ensure the Act remains aligned with evolving digital landscapes.

SECTION 12. SEVERABILITY

If any provision of this Act is found unconstitutional or unenforceable, all remaining provisions shall remain in full force and effect.

Closing Note for Policymakers

This model legislation is ambitious, but it is grounded in what developmental science, public-health history, and international precedent tell us: **children thrive in structured environments, and technology must now be structured accordingly.** Several countries around the world have already adopted policies that prohibit phones in schools, and while these actions are helpful, they barely scratch the surface of what kids need. Australia's decision to establish under-16 social media account restrictions shows that bold, developmentally based digital protections are not only possible, but already underway. CIPPSA builds on that momentum by addressing the broader risks associated with unrestricted smartphone access and offers a clear blueprint for the United States to protect children, strengthen families, support schools, and modernize its digital-safety framework. It is one piece of the exit plan our children deserve.

Chapter 11

This Way Out: Now It's Time to Climb

If you've made it to the end of this book, you've done something many people avoid: you stayed with the discomfort long enough to see the shape of the problem—and the shape of the solution. That matters. You are now a valuable part of the team we need to help kids find their way to wellness.

Because the situation we're in is not going to resolve itself through wishful thinking, one-off assemblies, a new curriculum, another app, another counseling referral, another short-term initiative, or another round of adults quietly hoping kids will "grow out of it." We have tried versions of all of those. We have held meetings. We have created plans. We have implemented programs. We have added services. We have urged kids to "make better choices." We have begged parents to "set limits." We have asked teachers to "do more with less." We have asked school counselors and clinicians to be both firefighters and architects. We have asked administrators to hold together systems that feel like they're under constant strain. We have asked legislators to catch up to technology that evolves faster than any policy cycle.

And meanwhile, the digital environment has continued to intensify—more persuasive, more ubiquitous, more socially binding, more difficult to resist, more profitable when it captures attention, and more capable of pulling a child away from sleep, movement, real-world connection, learning, and the slower rhythms that nervous systems require.

So here is the truth, as plainly and compassionately as I can say it:

We cannot continue to do more of the same.

Not because people haven't been trying.
Not because parents don't care.
Not because educators don't care.
Not because kids are weak or "different now."
Not because clinicians are failing.

Not because administrators are asleep at the wheel.
Not because lawmakers are heartless.

We can't continue to do more of the same because what we have been doing is very clearly not working.

The youth mental health crisis has reached epidemic proportions. With one in five youth experiencing a mental health challenge and no end in sight for reversing this escalating trend, we have no more time to waste [28]. If we go back to Malcolm Gladwell's *tipping point* concept for a moment, he states "An epidemic can be reversed, can be tipped, by tinkering with the smallest details of the immediate environment." [29] These small details are the hand and footholds I have illustrated in previous chapters—each of them grounded in science and targeted at the biological drivers of the crisis: the vicious cycle between sleep deprivation and digital overstimulation.

The hand and footholds are also based on the most effective behavior management strategy I know. It's not something I normally use first thing out of the gate when trying to correct behavior. Most behavior management begins with naming the behavior you want to change followed by several approaches that might include setting goals, developing incentive plans, or collaboratively solving problems. However, strategies like these are most effective when the person who needs to change their behavior has some awareness that their behavior is problematic. They may not want to change, but they can acknowledge their behavior is less than optimal.

In the case of the youth mental health crisis, there are two major players who lack the level of awareness needed for incentives or behavior plans to be effective.

- The first player is the current generation of youth who have been swimming in a sea of digital overstimulation their entire lives. They don't know anything different. They may realize they don't feel well, but since they never established a calm baseline, they have nothing to compare it to—and when they remove technology, they feel so awful, they can't see how reducing or removing it could possibly help.

- The second player includes the tech and social media companies. When you can sit in a Congressional hearing, in front of parents who have buried their children, and defend the safety of your products, there is clearly an inability or an unwillingness to acknowledge the need for change.

In both cases—whether we're talking about social media and tech companies or youth themselves—neither sees the problem clearly enough to rely on typical behavior management protocols.

This is why the main strategies I have recommended involve my go-to strategy when other behavior management strategies fail: that is to **remove the opportunity** for the person to engage in the behavior in the first place. This is why, for parents, my number one recommendation is to eliminate or disable devices in bedrooms at night. This small tinkering within the home environment **removes the opportunity** for youth to stay up all night, effectively wrecking both their sleep and their ability to cope with the stressors of modern life.

This is why, for educators, my number one recommendation is to eliminate phones from all schools. This small tinkering within the school environment **removes the opportunity** for students to:

- create or participate in drama during school hours
- be distracted by notifications
- scroll through content on their phone rather than engaging in the lesson at hand

For legislators and policymakers, this is why my number one recommendation is the CIPPSA bill, which **removes the opportunity** for social media/tech companies and online predators to harm our kids by completely removing online access to elementary-aged kids, and ensuring kids in middle and high school have been adequately prepared to navigate the online world before granting them independent access to it. While this is not a small tinkering of the environment, it is the most crucial part of the exit plan.

I recently spoke to a wise, Minneapolis-based technology teacher with a double master's degree who has been teaching technology for 30 plus years.

He told me there is no need for kids to be on devices or online to learn about technology. He said, we don't teach kids how to drive by giving them the keys to the car, sending them off by themselves, and saying, "Good luck—have fun." They first learn about cars while riding in the back seat, even before being allowed into the front passenger seat. After that, it's only after reaching a certain age that we allow kids behind the wheel, and even then, never alone. What do we do instead? We get them a learner's permit first, which requires an adult to be in the car with the youth, coaching them and guiding them, usually for a good six months before they can get their own license. Even then, we don't just give them a license. They must first pass both a written exam and a driver's test.

We should be exercising the same level of vigilance and accountability before we let our children roam free online. When we do otherwise, their curiosity—combined with a partially developed prefrontal cortex and limited impulse control, judgment, and problem-solving skills—lands them at the bottom of a well without the climbing skills needed to find their way out.

I recently had a 12-year-old tell me that her generation, Gen Alpha, is "really into doom scrolling and brain rot". Even more recently, I had a 17-year-old say, "Not too many people my age date, because dating is all about cheating and everything now is fake. Honestly, this is the worst generation to grow up in."

I can't tell you how sad this makes me to hear these things. I remember when I was 17. It was one of the best times of my life. I was still a kid, with the freedom to be a kid. There was so much to look forward to and part of that was the freedom of not yet being aware of the kinds of stress that come with adulthood- but now with deep fakes, online bullying, and social media algorithms, our kids are drowning in stress long before they reach adulthood.

The good news is that our kids are still reachable. We have seen evidence of their ability to adapt and change when adults choose to hold the line, and we have seen it despite the presence of the youth mental health crisis. For example:

- The dangerous hallways of the COVID-19 comeback are gone.
- Schools that have adopted phone-free policies are already giving us an indication that reducing online exposure and going phone-free in schools will help.
- From what I hear, students in phone-free schools are more engaged in their schoolwork and with each other.

That said, the kids are far from out of the well, and there still exists a powerful undercurrent that is pulling our kids down into the well in droves.

Throughout this book, I have shown you the hand and footholds I believe can help our youth climb out of the well, and everyone named in this book is part of the solution.

If you recognize yourself anywhere in these pages, you are now being invited to join the team.

Because that's what this requires: a team.

Not a perfect team. Not a team that agrees about everything, but a team nonetheless.

Not a Passing Phase

One of the reasons I wrote this book is that I don't think we're dealing with a small, temporary wave that will pass if we just "hang in there." I think we're dealing with a long-term shift in childhood and adolescence that we have not yet fully acknowledged as an emergency.

What I've described—sleep deprivation, rising anxiety, depressed mood, school refusal, dysregulation, attention fragmentation, social withdrawal, identity destabilization, and a profound sense of disconnection—has become normalized in too many settings. When something becomes common, we start calling it "typical." But typical does not mean healthy, and common does not mean acceptable.

And here's a key point: many of the youth struggling right now are not struggling because they are "broken." They are struggling because their bodies and brains are responding normally to an abnormal environment.

A developing nervous system is not designed to withstand:

- constant novelty and stimulation without recovery time
- social comparison and social threat, delivered 24/7
- the pressure to be "on" constantly, even in private spaces
- the replacement of movement and outdoor play with sedentary consumption
- chronic sleep restriction as a cultural norm
- content and interactions that bypass adult safeguards
- and a world where the most persuasive forces are often optimized to hold attention, not protect development

When we name it that way, something important happens: the problem becomes less personal and more solvable.

It stops being "What's wrong with these kids?"
And it becomes, "What are we doing to children—and what are we willing to change?"

That shift is essential, because it moves us from shame to strategy.

Compassionate Strategy in Action

I want to hold two truths together in this final chapter, because the moment we drop one, we lose our way.

Truth #1: People are doing the best they can with the information they have, in the circumstances they're in.

Truth #2: We have enough information now to know that many of our current patterns are harming children—and we must change them.

Keep in mind, we don't need everyone to do everything. We just need everyone to do something.

A lot of people read a book like this and may feel one of two things:

Relief: "Finally, someone said what I've been feeling."
Overwhelm: "This is too big. I can't fix this."

If you're feeling relief, good—use it. Relief is energy. It's the feeling of not being alone. It's the sense that there's a map.

If you're feeling overwhelmed, I will say this:

You are not responsible for fixing everything.

Just focus on doing your part. Keeping yourself focused on what you can control helps reduce the burden, and when you choose one meaningful action and repeat it, you become powerful again.

You might not be able to control what every other parent allows.
You might not be able to control what a platform does.
You might not be able to control what your school district implements.
You might not be able to control the pace of legislation.

But you can control:

- the boundaries you set in your home
- the consistency you bring as an educator
- the way you communicate as a clinician
- the policies you support as a leader
- the courage you bring as a lawmaker
- the norms you reinforce in your community
- the way you show up when it would be easier to avoid the conflict

And when enough people do that, something shifts. Culture shifts. Schools shift. Families shift. Policy shifts. The "normal" becomes something healthier.

That's what I mean when I say we are a team.

What "no more of the same" actually looks like

Let me color in the lines here because awareness matters, but awareness without action becomes its own form of avoidance.

"No more of the same" looks like:

- treating sleep, movement, hydration, nutrition, and connection as foundational—not optional
- creating boundaries that are firm enough to protect development and compassionate enough to preserve relationship
- building school structures that reduce digital usage during learning time
- redesigning community norms so children aren't socially punished for healthy limits
- shifting policy toward age-appropriate safeguards and transparent design
- supporting educators with realistic expectations and practical frameworks
- helping parents move from guilt to leadership
- helping kids reclaim real life—slow life—embodied life
- refusing to accept "this is just how it is now" as the final answer

No one can do all of that alone. That's why it's a team.

A Reminder of What We're Protecting

Sometimes in conversations about screens and phones and policy, we lose sight of the deeper things we're protecting.

We are protecting:

- a child's ability to sleep
- a teen's ability to think clearly
- a student's ability to tolerate discomfort without panic
- a young person's ability to build identity without constant comparison
- a nervous system's ability to experience calm
- the capacity to focus, learn, persist, and recover from mistakes
- the skills of real-world friendship—repair, empathy, patience, honesty
- the development of purpose and agency

- the ability to feel feelings without needing to escape them immediately
- the slow process of becoming a stable, resilient adult

When kids keep those capacities, they become the adults who can handle real life: relationships, work, citizenship, leadership, and the inevitable suffering that comes with being human.

This isn't about nostalgia. It's about development. It's about health. It's about the future.

Everyone is part of the solution

A team only works when each person knows their position and responsibilities as a team member, and everyone's part is different. When I played basketball, my job was to score points, rebound, and block shots, not to take the ball down the court. That job belonged to the point guard. When we all did our job, our team went undefeated.

This team will win when:

- Parents hold boundaries
- Educators keep structure
- Administrators protect staff and build workable systems
- Clinicians keep naming reality with compassion
- Policy makers create guardrails
- Communities stop rewarding harmful norms
- And kids experience adults who are steady enough to follow

You may be wondering how we are going to pull this off and how the youth will handle the changes. Based on my years of experience working with students, I am confident the youth will adjust. When the adults are onboard with the changes, the kids will be fine with them too. Will it be an adjustment for them? Sure, it will be. Growing pains are to be expected anytime you change the norm. Kids will test the limits to see if they'll stick, but once they know the change is here to stay, they adapt to the new expectations and it just becomes part of the culture.

The challenge will be to get all of the adults on board first. For those of you who say, "Nope, we're too deep in this, we can't undo what's already done," I'll say what my grandmother used to say anytime I told her I couldn't do something: "Then you don't want it bad enough." For those who say the kids won't cooperate with this plan, I say: "If the adults clearly show they are okay with the changes, the kids will be okay too."

We saw this very clearly coming back from COVID-19. It was the adults who didn't want to return to school out of fear that the students wouldn't comply with the mask and social distancing guidelines. Well, they did. There were very few concerns, and most concerns over masks had to do with sensory issues and not because a student was refusing or had oppositional behavior. Masks and social distancing were the expectation, and the students fell in line.

I truly believe if you picked up this book and have reached the end, you were already concerned about our kids. You may have reached out for help or tried to help in your own way. And clearly there have been millions, if not billions of dollars earmarked to address the youth mental health crisis. As I have stated throughout this book, we are not in the position we are in now because of lack of trying, lack of concern, or a lack of resources.

I would argue that we have been throwing money and resources in the wrong direction, toward crisis response and downstream interventions. I am advocating for us to change our focus and target our efforts upstream at the root cause of the problem. By eliminating early, unnecessary, and overexposure to digital devices, we are now targeting the upstream causes that land our kids at the bottom of the well. It's a fundamental paradigm shift that needs to happen if we are to end this crisis. Let's quit putting Band-Aids on gaping wounds and stop our youth from getting injured in the first place.

Real hope is built when enough of us do our part. You don't need to overhaul your entire life in one day. Pick a few actions, hold them, and build.

A Mobilizing Checklist You Can Actually Use

If you're a parent or caregiver

Choose one sleep boundary you can enforce consistently this week.
Choose one device boundary (time, location, or overnight storage) that's clear and predictable.
Choose one replacement activity (movement, connection, or skill-building) and schedule it.
Choose one repair moment: a calm conversation with your child that separates them from the problem ("I'm on your team.").
Choose one ally: another parent you can coordinate with.

If you're an educator or school staff member

Choose one predictable routine to strengthen (entry, transitions, closure).
Choose one regulation support to normalize (movement break, quiet reset, structured breathing).
Choose one relationship action: a check-in with one student who is slipping.
Choose one policy conversation you will initiate or join (devices, sleep education, family partnership).

If you're a clinician

Assess foundations (sleep/movement/hydration/nutrition/connection) as part of the treatment plan.
Choose one family boundary to support and make it sustainable.
Choose one language shift that reduces shame and increases agency.
Choose one community voice opportunity (even small) to widen the conversation beyond the therapy room.

If you're a policymaker/leader

Choose one protection priority you will advance (age safeguards, transparency, enforceable device policies).
Choose one listening session with educators/clinicians/families to ground policy in reality.
Choose one prevention investment you will advocate for, not just crisis response.
Choose one public message that frames this as child safety and development—not blame.

If you're a community member
Support one parent who sets limits (encouragement matters).
Create one screen-light gathering opportunity (a walk, a game night, a club, a sports meet-up).
Model one device behavior you'd want a child to copy.

The future is still available

One of the most painful things about this crisis is the sense that we've "lost" something—childhood, joy, peace, focus, resilience.

But the truth is: those things are not gone. They're buried.

They're buried under sleep deprivation.
They're buried under overstimulation.
They're buried under constant comparison.
They're buried under stress and disconnection.
They're buried under the belief that we can't change anything.

When we remove the conditions that are harming kids—and replace them with what kids actually need—those capacities will return.

Not overnight. Not magically. Not without resistance.

But they will return.

I have seen it.

I have watched kids soften again when they finally sleep.
I have watched anxiety reduce when the nervous system stops being constantly hijacked.
I have watched attention improve when the environment becomes less fragmented.
I have watched parents reconnect with their children when boundaries become consistent and conflict becomes less constant.
I have watched teachers reclaim their classrooms when structure becomes enforceable and relationships become central again.
I have watched students discover that they can tolerate boredom, tolerate

discomfort, and even enjoy a life that is not constantly mediated by a screen.

The future is still available—but it requires us to stop pretending nothing needs to change.

What to remember when you close this book

If you forget details, statistics, frameworks, and step lists, I want you to remember these truths:

We cannot continue to do more of the same.
Everyone named in this book is part of the solution.
The only person you can control is yourself.
If everyone does their part, we can do this.
We are a team—and our mission is the safety of our children and the future of our world.

That is the exit plan.

Not a single rule. Not a single program. Not a single hero.

A team. A map. A shared commitment.

And a willingness to act.

Appendix A: Methods & Ethics

This book was created through a collaboration between me and an AI research and editing assistant. Because the subject is youth mental health, I chose to ground every chapter in a clear ethical framework.

Human dignity and autonomy
I treat every child, teen, and adult in these pages as a whole person with inherent worth and a right to participate in decisions that affect them. When I describe systems, I try not to lose sight of the individual young person at the center.

Do good, avoid harm, and protect rights
Recommendations in this book aim to improve wellbeing while minimizing harm. I actively consider potential downsides—stigma, over-surveillance, coercive practices—and lean toward voluntary, least-restrictive, and rights-respecting solutions.

Justice and equity
Youth mental health does not exist in a vacuum. Whenever possible, I ask: Who benefits? Who is burdened? Who is being left out? I pay special attention to the experiences of marginalized and underserved communities.

Transparency and privacy
The AI assistant helped organize research, language, and structure, but it does not replace professional judgment, lived experience, or ethical reflection. Examples are de-identified or composite to protect privacy.

Collaborative humility
Ethics is not a one-time checklist. As research evolves and communities speak, my views may also evolve. I invite readers to treat this book as the start of an ongoing conversation about how to protect and strengthen youth mental health with compassion, courage, and fairness.

Appendix B: Letter to the Surgeon General

January 4, 2022

Dear Dr. Vivek Murthy,
I am writing in response to your Youth Mental Health Advisory. First, I want to thank you for disseminating your report. It includes a lot of valuable information. That said, I have two additional recommendations that I hope you will seriously consider. These recommendations, along with my rationale for each, are based on my 30-years of clinical training and experience working with youth.

1. **Consider attaching a surgeon general's warning on the packaging of all electronic devices, particularly those that can access the internet.**
    - These devices are designed to addict the user, and addiction compromises youth mental health.
    - Unmonitored internet access exposes youth to online bullying, violent pornography, trafficking, and victimization, all of which compromise youth mental health
    - Excessive or poorly timed use of these devices compromises sleep quality, which in turn compromises youth mental health.
    - A warning of this type sends a clear message to parents that they need to monitor, reduce, and/or eliminate their child's electronic usage.
2. **Consider supporting a bill to establish 16 as the legal age to own a smartphone. A bill like this would**:
    - Send a clear message that these devices are potentially addictive and harmful to the developing brain. Similar to cigarettes and alcohol, smartphone usage should be delayed to avoid compromising children's development and overall wellbeing.
    - Send a clear message that these devices require a level of maturity and responsibility to use them, similar to driving a car or owning a gun.
    - Provide more substantial motivation to companies who design smartphones (and other electronic devices) to

develop effective safeguards if they are to access the youth market in the future.

- Give parents the leverage and support they need to transition their kids to a flip phone, which is all youth really need.
- Remove smartphone distractions in all K-8 schools and allow students to better focus on schoolwork.
- Help reduce juvenile cases of sexting and youth distribution of child pornography.
- Most importantly, make an immediate and significant impact on youth mental health.

Mental health initiatives such as additional social-emotional programming, mental health training for lay people and research on electronics are still needed, but these initiatives will take time; time that we do not have. We are clearly at a critical juncture. As you mentioned in your advisory, our children are dying in record numbers. Consequently, we need interventions that can significantly impact the youth mental health crisis in a positive direction. In the interest of our children's safety and wellbeing, I believe there is enough evidence to warrant restricting youth access to smartphones and providing a universal warning on all other electronic devices until further research can be conducted. In my opinion, the burden should be on the researchers to provide enough evidence to reconsider increasing access to our youth. The stakes are too high to do otherwise.

Youth mental health is my life's work and I would welcome the opportunity to share more insights and data should you or your team wish to contact me.

Respectfully submitted,
Kathleen Mackenzie, EdD, LICSW

Endnotes

1. Substance Abuse and Mental Health Services Administration. (2014). Projections of national expenditures for treatment of mental and substance use disorders, 2010–2020. U.S. Department of Health and Human Services; Centers for Disease Control and Prevention. (2024). Youth Risk Behavior Survey data summary & trends report: 2013–2023. U.S. Department of Health and Human Services; Bommersbach, T. J., Rosenheck, S., Rhee, T. G., Schneider, A. L., & Ranney, M. L. (2023). National trends in mental health-related emergency department visits among children, adolescents, and young adults in the United States, 2011–2020. JAMA, 329(12), 1034–1042.

2. Lipton, B. H. (2005). The biology of belief: Unleashing the power of consciousness, matter & miracles. Mountain of Love/Elite Books; National Institutes of Health. (2016). Stem cell basics. NIH Stem Cell Information (archived).

3. National Human Genome Research Institute. (2020, November 17). Epigenomics. National Institutes of Health; Feil, R., & Fraga, M. F. (2012). Epigenetics and the environment: Emerging patterns and implications. Nature Reviews Genetics, 13, 97–109.

4. Morrow, A. (2014). Med-free bipolar: Thrive naturally with the Med Free Method. Pottenger Publishing.

5. Walker, M. (2017). Why we sleep: Unlocking the power of sleep and dreams. Scribner.

6. Cleveland Clinic. (2024, March 8). Cerebral hypoxia.

7. Begley, S. (2002, December 9). How long can the average person survive without water? Scientific American.

8. Ross, J. J. (1965). Neurological findings after prolonged sleep deprivation. Archives of Neurology, 12(4), 399–403.

9. Sifferlin, A. (2004, November 8). How long can a person survive without food? Scientific American.

10. Holt-Lunstad, J., Smith, T. B., Baker, M., Harris, T., & Stephenson, D. (2015). Loneliness and social isolation as risk factors for mortality: A meta-analytic review. Perspectives on Psychological Science, 10(2), 227–237;

Office of the U.S. Surgeon General. (2023). Our epidemic of loneliness and isolation: The U.S. Surgeon General's advisory on the healing effects of social connection and community. U.S. Department of Health and Human Services.

11. Mandsager, K., Harb, S., Cremer, P., Phelan, D., Nissen, S. E., & Jaber, W. (2018). Association of cardiorespiratory fitness with long-term mortality among adults undergoing exercise treadmill testing. JAMA Network Open, 1(6), e183605.

12. Riebl, S. K., & Davy, B. M. (2013). The hydration equation: Update on water balance and cognitive performance. ACSM's Health & Fitness Journal, 17(6), 21–28.

13. Insel, T. R., & Young, L. J. (2001). The neurobiology of attachment. Nature Reviews Neuroscience, 2, 129–136.

14. Berridge, K.C., Venier, I.L., & Robinson, T.E. (1989). Taste reactivity analysis of 6-hydroxydopamine-induced aphagia: Implications for arousal and anhedonia Hypotheses of dopamine function. Behavioral Neuroscience, 103(1), 36-45.

15. Baglioni, C., Battagliese, G., Feige, B., Spiegelhalder, K., Nissen, C., Voderholzer, U., Lombardo, C., & Riemann, D. (2011). Insomnia as a predictor of depression: A meta-analytic evaluation of longitudinal epidemiological studies. Journal of Affective Disorders, 135(1–3), 10–19; Yoo, S. S., Gujar, N., Hu, P., Jolesz, F. A., & Walker, M. P. (2007). The human emotional brain without sleep—A prefrontal amygdala disconnect. Current Biology, 17, R877–R878.

16. Rasch, B., & Born, J. (2013). About sleep's role in memory. Physiological Reviews, 93(2), 681–766.

17. National Institute of General Medical Sciences. (2025, May 20). Circadian rhythms. National Institutes of Health.

18. Paruthi, S., Brooks, L. J., D'Ambrosio, C., Hall, W. A., Kotagal, S., Lloyd, R. M., Malow, B. A., Maski, K., Nichols, C., Quan, S. F., Rosen, C. L., Troester, M. M., & Wise, M. S. (2016). Recommended amount of sleep for pediatric populations: A consensus statement of the American Academy of Sleep Medicine. Journal of Clinical Sleep Medicine, 12(6), 785–786.

19. Mackenzie, K. (2022, March 16). Could sleep help end the youth mental health crisis? Psychology Today.

20. Greene, R. W. (2014). Lost at school: Why our kids with behavioral challenges are falling through the cracks and how we can help them. Scribner.

21. Culture Reframed Parents Program. (2021). Resource links. https://parents.culturereframed.org/resource-links/; Common Sense Media. (2018). Family media agreement. https://www.commonsensemedia.org/family-media-agreement

22. Paruthi, S., Brooks, L. J., D'Ambrosio, C., Hall, W. A., Kotagal, S., Lloyd, R. M., Malow, B. A., Maski, K., Nichols, C., Quan, S. F., Rosen, C. L., Troester, M. M., & Wise, M. S. (2016). Recommended amount of sleep for pediatric populations: A consensus statement of the American Academy of Sleep Medicine. Journal of Clinical Sleep Medicine, 12(6), 785–786.

23. American Academy of Pediatrics. (2014). School start times for adolescents. Pediatrics, 134(3), 642–649.

24. U.S. Environmental Protection Agency. (2018). 3Ts for reducing lead in drinking water in schools and child care facilities (Revised manual).

25. U.S. Department of Agriculture, Food and Nutrition Service. (2022). School meals: Healthy meals for kids.

26. Willis, J. (2006). Research-based strategies to ignite student learning: Insights from a neurologist and classroom teacher. Association for Supervision and Curriculum Development.

27. Centers for Disease Control and Prevention. (2025, June 5). Data and statistics on children's mental health. U.S. Department of Health and Human Services.

28. Centers for Disease Control and Prevention. (2025, June 5). Data and statistics on children's mental health. U.S. Department of Health and Human Services.

29. Gladwell, M. (2000). The tipping point: How little things can make a big difference (with a new afterword by the author). Little, Brown and Company.

Selected Sources

American Academy of Pediatrics. (2014). School start times for adolescents. Pediatrics, 134(3), 642–649.

Baglioni, C., Battagliese, G., Feige, B., Spiegelhalder, K., Nissen, C., Voderholzer, U., Lombardo, C., & Riemann, D. (2011). Insomnia as a predictor of depression: A meta-analytic evaluation of longitudinal epidemiological studies. Journal of Affective Disorders, 135(1–3), 10–19.

Bommersbach, T. J., Rosenheck, S., Rhee, T. G., Schneider, A. L., & Ranney, M. L. (2023). National trends in mental health-related emergency department visits among children, adolescents, and young adults in the United States, 2011–2020. JAMA, 329(12), 1034–1042.

Centers for Disease Control and Prevention. (2024). Youth Risk Behavior Survey data summary & trends report: 2013–2023. U.S. Department of Health and Human Services.

Centers for Disease Control and Prevention. (2025, June 5). Data and statistics on children's mental health. U.S. Department of Health and Human Services.

Culture Reframed Parents Program. (2021). Resource links.

Feil, R., & Fraga, M. F. (2012). Epigenetics and the environment: Emerging patterns and implications. Nature Reviews Genetics, 13, 97–109.

Greene, R. W. (2014). Lost at school: Why our kids with behavioral challenges are falling through the cracks and how we can help them. Scribner.

Holt-Lunstad, J., Smith, T. B., Baker, M., Harris, T., & Stephenson, D. (2015). Loneliness and social isolation as risk factors for mortality: A meta-analytic review. Perspectives on Psychological Science, 10(2), 227–237.

Insel, T. R., & Young, L. J. (2001). The neurobiology of attachment. Nature Reviews Neuroscience, 2, 129–136.

Lipton, B. H. (2005). The biology of belief: Unleashing the power of consciousness, matter & miracles. Mountain of Love/Elite Books.

Mackenzie, K. (2022, March 16). Could sleep help end the youth mental health crisis? Psychology Today.

Mandsager, K., Harb, S., Cremer, P., Phelan, D., Nissen, S. E., & Jaber, W. (2018). Association of cardiorespiratory fitness with long-term mortality among adults undergoing exercise treadmill testing. JAMA Network Open, 1(6), e183605.

Morrow, A. (2014). Med-free bipolar: Thrive naturally with the Med Free Method. Pottenger Publishing.

National Institute of General Medical Sciences. (2025, May 20). Circadian rhythms. National Institutes of Health.

Office of the U.S. Surgeon General. (2023). Our epidemic of loneliness and isolation: The U.S. Surgeon General's advisory on the healing effects of social connection and community. U.S. Department of Health and Human Services.

Rasch, B., & Born, J. (2013). About sleep's role in memory. Physiological Reviews, 93(2), 681–766.

Riebl, S. K., & Davy, B. M. (2013). The hydration equation: Update on water balance and cognitive performance. ACSM's Health & Fitness Journal, 17(6), 21–28.

Sifferlin, A. (2004, November 8). How long can a person survive without food? Scientific American.

Substance Abuse and Mental Health Services Administration. (2014). Projections of national expenditures for treatment of mental and substance use disorders, 2010–2020. U.S. Department of Health and Human Services.

U.S. Department of Agriculture, Food and Nutrition Service. (2022). School meals: Healthy meals for kids.

Walker, M. (2017). Why we sleep: Unlocking the power of sleep and dreams. Scribner.

Willis, J. (2006). Research-based strategies to ignite student learning: Insights from a neurologist and classroom teacher. Association for Supervision and Curriculum Development.

Acknowledgments

I am grateful to have chosen a career that attracts people who deeply care for kids and families. This book was shaped by the collective wisdom shared with me by the countless colleagues I have worked with over the course of my career. I want to give a particular thanks to Jarred Varao who stepped into my role when I retired. Knowing the work was in capable hands helped me leave with peace and focus fully on writing this book. My hope is that it ultimately brings more support to those still working in schools.

I want to thank my early readers, each of whom strengthened this book in their own way: Dr. Kristen Lee for her publishing guidance, meticulous feedback, a generous foreword, and years of enthusiastic nudges to write a book; Annie Lanzillotto for her visceral writing style; Barbara Kaplan, my first clinical supervisor after graduate school; Cathy Rutkowski for our shared mission to eliminate child victimization; Cara Bean for helping kids find their voice through art; Darcy Lee for her life-saving work at the Samaritans; and last but certainly not least, my sister Kirsteen Mitchell for her no-nonsense feedback that has been so important to my writing. Thank you to my team at Punch Creatives for supporting the book launch and to Jody Barna for translating the image in my head into the beautiful cover illustration.

I also want to acknowledge two important mentors in my work with youth; Dr. Marlene Rodriques (may she rest in peace) and John Crocker, whose leadership in school-based mental health has guided my thinking. Thank you to the youth and families for their trust in me; to my partner, David Zimmel, who helps me fully unplug; and to my parents who have provided me with a lifetime of unconditional love and support. I love and appreciate you all.

www.ingramcontent.com/pod-product-compliance
Lightning Source LLC
LaVergne TN
LVHW011633200926
848484LV00014B/2584/J